EVERYTHING YOU NEED TO KNOW ABOUT

FRENCH HOMEWORK

EVERYTHING YOU NEED TO KNOW ABOUT

FRENCH HOMEWORK

MARIE TURCOTTE

Scholastic Canada Ltd.
Toronto New York London Auckland Sydney
Mexico City New Delhi Hong Kong Buenos Aires

Scholastic Canada Ltd.
604 King Street West, Toronto, Ontario M5V 1E1, Canada

Scholastic Inc.
557 Broadway, New York, NY 10012, USA

Scholastic Australia Pty Limited
PO Box 579, Gosford, NSW 2250, Australia

Scholastic New Zealand Limited
Private Bag 94407, Greenmount, Auckland, New Zealand

Scholastic Ltd.
Eusten House, 24 Eversholt Street, London NW1 1DB, UK

Interior design: Bennett Gewirtz, Gewirtz Graphics, Inc.
Illustrations: Tyrone McCarthy, www.tyronemccarthy.com: p. 77 (all);
Adam Wood: cover, p. 65 (bottom); www.mikecarterstudio.com: p. 12, p. 13 (both),
p. 20 (both), p. 25, p. 28 (both), p. 32, p. 33, p. 35, p. 36 (bottom), p. 38, p. 41 (all),
p. 44, p. 45, p. 47, p. 48, p. 49, p. 52, p. 60, p. 62, p. 65 (top), p. 69 (both), p. 72, p. 80
Photographs: Alfredo Aldai/epa/Corbis: p. 16 (top); © Dan Breckwoldt/istockphoto: p. 21; The Canadian Press/Steve White: p. 4 (top); Canadian Space Agency: p. 18; Carnaval de Québec: p. 9; Commission du tourisme acadien du Canada atlantique: p. 11; © Julie de Leseleuc/istockphoto: p. 3 (bottom); Dominique et compagnie: p. 15 (top); Festival du Voyageur Inc.: p. 10 (both); Chris Iwanowski: p. 12; Trevor Kazakoff: p. 6; Le chandail © 1980 National Film Board of Canada. All rights reserved.: p. 15 (bottom); Jerome Prevost/Corbis: p. 17; Andreas Sundgren, flickr.com/photos/asundgren: p. 16 (bottom); Tourism New Brunswick: p. 4 (bottom), p. 5;
© Tony Tremblay/istockphoto: p. 3 (top); © Eric Wheater/Lonely Planet Images: p. 7 (bottom)

Library and Archives Canada Cataloguing in Publication
Turcotte, Marie

Everything you need to know about French homework / Marie Turcotte.
Includes some text in French.

ISBN 978-0-545-99011-0

1. French language—Grammar—Problems, exercises, etc.—Juvenile literature.
2. French language—Composition and exercises—Juvenile literature. I. Title.

PC2129.E5 T87 2009   448.2   C2009-900521-2

ISBN-10 0-545-99011-4

Project development, editing, design, and layout: First Folio Resource Group Inc.
Reviewers: Marina Marukhnyak, Department of French, University of Toronto; Brenda McKinley, Halton District School Board; Dr. Jeffrey Steele, Department of French, University of Toronto

Copyright © 2009 by Scholastic Canada Ltd.
All rights reserved.

No part of this publication may be reproduced or stored in a retrieval system, or transmitted in any form or by any means, electronic, mechanical, recording, or otherwise, without written permission of the publisher, Scholastic Canada Ltd., 604 King Street West, Toronto, Ontario M5V 1E1, Canada. In the case of photocopying or other reprographic copying, a licence must be obtained from Access Copyright (Canadian Copyright Licensing Agency), 1 Yonge Street, Suite 800, Toronto, Ontario M5E 1E5 (1-800-893-5777).

10 9 8 7 6 5 4 3 2 1   Printed in Canada   09 10 11 12 13 14 15 16 17 18

Contents

Introduction vii

Part 1. Why Learn French?

1. Living in French in Canada 2
   Quebec
   Other Provinces
   French in Canada: A Historical Background
   French Around the World

2. French-Canadian Culture 9
   Festivals
   Food
   The Arts

3. More Famous French Canadians 17
   IT'S A WRAP! 19
   ADULTS CAN HELP 22

Part 2. The Letter

Letters and Sounds 23
   The Alphabet
   TRY THIS!
   French Accents
   TRY THIS!
   Special Letter Combinations
   TRY THIS!
   Special Consonants
   TRY THIS!
   Pronouncing Final Consonants
   TRY THIS!

IT'S A WRAP! 30
ADULTS CAN HELP 30

Part 3. Parts of Speech

1. Nouns 31
Common and Proper Nouns
Masculine and Feminine Nouns
TRY THIS!
Singular and Plural Nouns
TRY THIS!

2. Pronouns 38
Subject Pronouns

3. Adjectives 40
Masculine and Feminine Adjectives
Singular and Plural Adjectives
TRY THIS!
Possessive Adjectives
TRY THIS!
Interrogative Adjectives
Placement of Adjectives

4. Verbs 44
ER, IR, and RE Verbs
TRY THIS!
Common Irregular Verbs
TRY THIS!
The Imperative
TRY THIS!

5. Adverbs. 52
Types of Adverbs
TRY THIS!

6. Small But Important Words 54
Prepositions
Conjunctions
Interjections

7. Putting It All Together 57
The Sentence
Making a Sentence Negative
TRY THIS!
Asking a Question
TRY THIS!

IT'S A WRAP! 59

ADULTS CAN HELP 59

Part 4. How to Communicate in French

1. Listening 60
Strategies Good Listeners Use
Things to Listen To
TRY THIS!

2. Reading 64
Strategies Good Readers Use
Things to Read
TRY THIS!

3. Speaking. 66
Strategies Good Speakers Use
Intonation
TRY THIS!

4. Writing 72
Strategies Good Writers Use
TRY THIS!

IT'S A WRAP! 79

ADULTS CAN HELP 80

Part 5. Building Your Vocabulary

1. Pronunciation Guide 81
2. Commonly Used Words 84

Appendix 1:
Useful Resources 96

Appendix 2:
Answer Key 98

Index 103

Introduction

You're studying French at school and you'd like to practise at home. Maybe you need help with homework or you just want to learn a little more about the language. Either way you need some help, but no one in your family speaks French very well and you're not sure what to do. Where can you go for help?

In *Everything You Need to Know About French Homework*, you'll find a wealth of information about the French language, including answers to some of the most commonly asked questions.

What Questions Does This Book Answer?

- What do French Canadians eat?
  - ► See **Food** on pages 12–13.
- Which French Canadians are famous in Canada and around the world?
  - ► See **The Arts** and **More Famous French Canadians** on pages 14–19.
- How do I pronounce letters and words in French?
  - ► See **Letters and Sounds** on pages 23–30, **Speaking** on pages 66–71, and **Pronunciation Guide** on pages 81–83.
- How can I tell if a word is masculine or feminine?
  - ► See **Masculine and Feminine Nouns** on pages 32–35 and **Masculine and Feminine Adjectives** on page 40.
- How do I make words plural?
  - ► See **Singular and Plural Nouns** on pages 36–37 and **Singular and Plural Adjectives** on page 40.

INTRODUCTION

- Once I know a verb, how do I use it in a sentence?
  - See **Verbs** on pages 44–51 and **Putting It All Together** on pages 57–59.
- Where can I find French in my community?
  - See **Listening** on page 60 and **Reading** on page 64.
- How can I learn to understand people when they speak French?
  - See **Strategies Good Listeners Use** on pages 61–62.
- What strategies can I use to help me understand what I read in French?
  - See **Strategies Good Readers Use** on pages 64–65.
- How do I say things like the days of the week, months of the year, and names of our provinces and territories?
  - See **Commonly Used Words** on pages 84–95.

Each section of this book has examples, illustrations, and short exercises called *Try This!* and *It's a Wrap!* so you can practise what you learn. You can do the exercises in your notebook, then check many of the answers in Appendix 2: Answer Key. Read several pages at a time or simply look up what you need to know right now.

What is the *Everything You Need to Know About . . . Homework* Series?

The *Everything You Need to Know About . . . Homework* series is a set of unique reference resources written especially to answer the homework questions of fourth-, fifth-, and sixth-graders. The series provides ready information to answer commonly asked homework questions in a variety of subjects. Here you'll find facts, charts, definitions, and explanations, complete with examples and illustrations that will supplement schoolwork colourfully, clearly, and comprehensively.

A Note to Parents

Your child has started studying French at school and is probably excited at the prospect of learning a new language. But you may be somewhat nervous about helping your child because you don't know the language or you haven't used it in years. This is natural and it's a situation that many parents face.

The most important thing you can do to is to create an environment that encourages your child to learn French. You may wish to visit your local library or bookstore together and look for French books, CDs, DVDs, or videos that your child can use at home. Many DVDs have both a French and English language option, so you and your child can watch favourite movies and television programs in French, or you can turn on the subtitles while watching in English. Together, you might read the labels on cereal boxes or watch television on a local French TV network. You can use the Internet to download children's podcasts and watch or listen to them with your child. Encourage your child to watch and listen many times; at first he or she may have problems understanding the content, but it will become easier with practice.

You may also want to serve some French-Canadian foods to your family, perhaps as part of a French culture day. For example, you could make a *tourtière* (a meat pie), pea soup, or crêpes. There are many good recipes on the Internet. The first section of this book contains a great deal of information about French culture that you can share with your child.

If you know people who speak French, ask them to speak French to your child whenever possible so that he or she gets used to the sounds of the language. French people have different accents and they speak at different speeds, depending on where they come from, so it's important to expose your child to a variety of voices. Teachers tend to speak more slowly because they want their students to be able to follow along; native speakers usually speak much more quickly than non-native speakers.

With your child, take part in French activities, such as concerts or festivals, that are in or near your community. If you're able to travel to Quebec or to French communities in other parts of the country, involve your child in planning the trip. Together, you can research your destination and decide what sights you'd like to see and what activities and events you'd like to participate in.

Students will learn French the same way infants learn a language — first they'll speak in individual words and in short order they'll learn to pronounce full sentences. Initially, they'll repeat constantly, but eventually they'll learn to put together their own sentences. Everything they do is modelled by the teacher. This modelling and building from first steps helps students learn to think in French. People who are fluent in a second language do not translate their thoughts from their first language; instead, they learn to think in their second language.

Parents who don't speak French are sometimes tempted to help their children with their French homework by asking them to translate from English to French. Doing this will frustrate students, since this isn't the way they're learning French at school. Try to resist the temptation. On the other hand, some strategic translation is necessary as we learn a language, and English translations of many common French words are provided in this book.

Further suggestions for helping your child as he or she learns French are provided at the end of each section of this book in *Adults Can Help*. Learn along with your child; by doing so, you show your child how important it is to learn a second language. Enjoy the experience together!

Part 1: Why Learn French?

Chapter 1: Living in French in Canada

French is not just a subject that people in Canada learn in school; it's part of our heritage. Canada is officially a bilingual country, where both English and French are recognized as official languages.

The majority of Canada's Francophones live in Quebec, Ontario, and New Brunswick, although there are Francophone communities in every province and territory. Learning French allows you to speak with people in all these places and in French-speaking countries around the world.

Quebec

French is the only official language of Quebec, though many people in Quebec speak English too. These people are usually bilingual — that is, they speak both English and French.

Most students in Quebec go to French schools and French universities. People speak French in offices, stores, and restaurants. If you call a taxi in Quebec, you'll be expected to give the address in French. If you order concert tickets, you'll speak in French too.

Other Provinces

French is also one of the official languages of New Brunswick, Nunavut, and the Northwest Territories. Other provinces and territories also offer services in French. In some provinces, you can speak English or French in the legislature and in courts. You can go to French schools and universities too.

WHY LEARN FRENCH?

Quebec City is Quebec's capital. It was founded in 1608 by French explorer Samuel de Champlain and is the only remaining fortified city in North America. The old city, known as Vieux Québec, is surrounded by almost 4.6 kilometres of defensive walls and gates.

Both French and English are spoken on the streets of Ottawa and on Parliament Hill, the seat of Canada's government. Being able to speak Canada's two official languages makes it easier to get many government jobs.

3

Founded in 1642, Montreal is Canada's second-largest city and one of the largest French-speaking cities in the world. Many of its historic buildings still stand today, especially in Old Montreal. Tourists wander the narrow streets, admiring the architecture, shopping, eating in restaurants, and watching performances in the main square.

Spread across Atlantic Canada are regions with French roots, language, and culture. These regions are known as l'Acadie, or Acadia. Festivals celebrating Acadian heritage take place throughout the area, including this one in Caraquet, in northeastern New Brunswick.

French in Canada: A Historical Background

According to the 2006 Canadian census, there are 6 817 655 people in Canada whose first language is French. Most of them were born in Canada, and the others moved here from French-speaking countries around the world. Let's take a look at how this came to be.

The First Francophones in Canada

The first Francophone to come to Canada was the French explorer Jacques Cartier. He made three trips to Canada: in 1534, 1535, and 1541. Over the course of those years, he explored the land that is now Newfoundland, Prince Edward Island, the Magdalen Islands, and the Gaspé Peninsula. In Gaspé, he planted a cross with the French royal coat of arms on it to symbolize that he was taking possession of the territory on behalf of the King of France. The coat of arms included a fleur-de-lis, which looks like a fancy lily or iris flower. The fleur-de-lis was a symbol of French royalty.

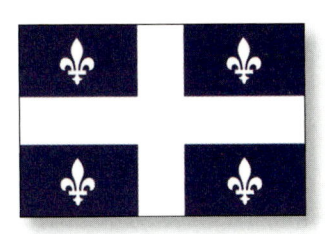

Quebec's flag is a white cross surrounded by four fleurs-de-lis on a blue background.

The Village Historique Acadien, in New Brunswick, recreates Acadian life between 1770 and 1949. The Acadians are descendants of the original Francophone families who colonized what is now Nova Scotia, New Brunswick, and Prince Edward Island. Acadian families are also spread out in Louisiana and other parts of the United States.

WHY LEARN FRENCH?

In the 1800s, St. Boniface, Manitoba became a religious centre for French communities in western Canada. It is still home to a thriving French community.

Over the next two centuries, other people came from France to settle in Canada. Voyageurs and coureurs de bois mapped out the country, travelled the waterways, and set up trading posts with Aboriginal peoples. Many Catholic priests and nuns came to look after the educational and spiritual aspects of colonists' lives. In your Social Studies classes, you will learn about some of the French explorers who travelled to our country.

Francophones New to Canada

Even today, people immigrate to Canada from other French-speaking countries such as Haiti, Senegal, Rwanda, and the Democratic Republic of the Congo. Many of these immigrants settle in Quebec or in French-speaking communities in other parts of the country.

French Around the World

More than 200 million people around the world speak French. Many of the countries where people speak French today were colonized by France centuries ago, just as Canada was.

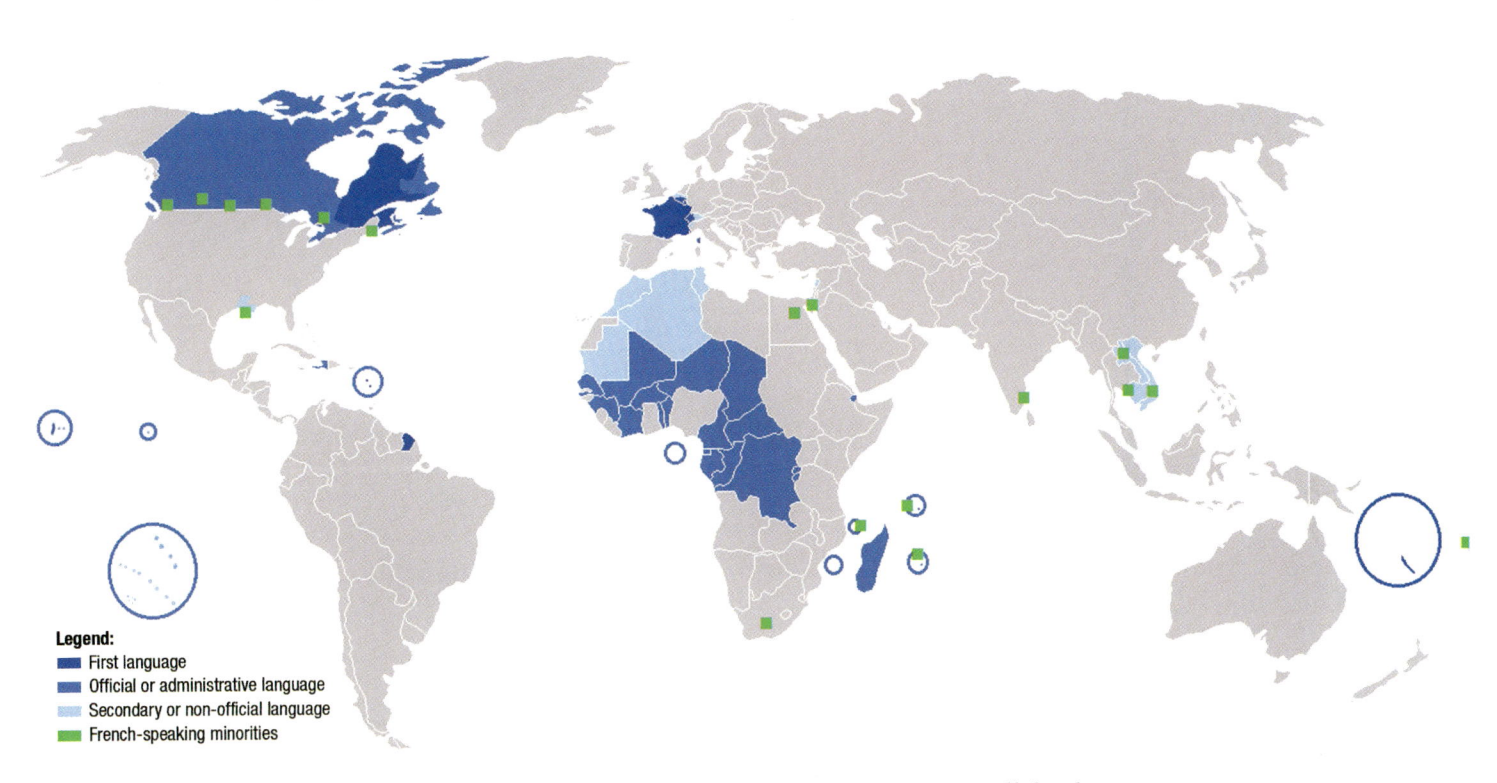

Legend:
- First language
- Official or administrative language
- Secondary or non-official language
- French-speaking minorities

Whether you travel to Haiti, Vietnam, Rwanda, or Switzerland, you will find people to talk to in French.

People in Haiti, seen here riding on a decorated bus known as a tap-tap bus, speak both French and Haitian Creole. French is used mainly in school, government, and business, while Haitian Creole is the language that most people speak in their day-to-day lives.

WHY LEARN FRENCH?

Legend:
- Member
- Observer

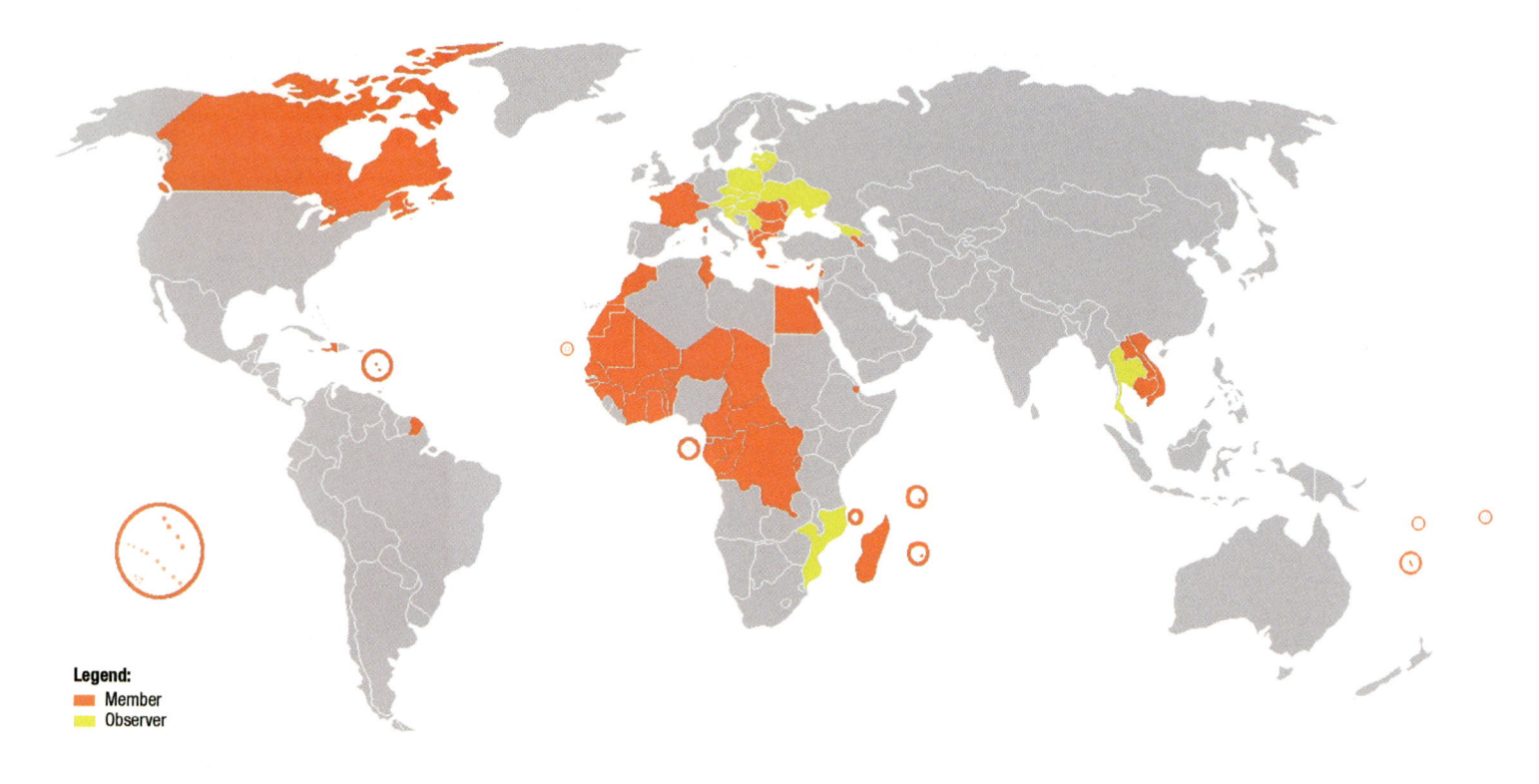

This map shows the countries and governments that are part of the Organisation internationale de la Francophonie (OIF).

The OIF

In 1970, an organization of French-speaking countries was founded to discuss Francophone issues around the world. It is called the Organisation internationale de la Francophonie (OIF). It includes representatives from 70 countries and governments. The OIF meets every two years to discuss issues related to French language and culture; peace, democracy, and human rights; education; the economy; and the environment. For example, the OIF might discuss how to improve the lives of children living in poverty or promote human rights in its member countries. Usually, the prime ministers and presidents of the member countries attend this summit. The premiers of Quebec and New Brunswick have attended too.

Chapter 2: French-Canadian Culture

Look around you — in your home, in your town, on TV, and in schools and other buildings. No matter where you live in Canada, you will see evidence of French-Canadian culture.

The first people to arrive from France in 1534 brought with them their music, foods, and holiday traditions. More recent French-speaking immigrants have brought their traditions too. All of these have become part of the French-Canadian culture.

Festivals

French-Canadian festivals celebrate historic events, people's heritage and ancestry, religion, and the seasons. Many festivals take place in the winter, just like the celebrations of early French settlers. Since they could not farm or fish in the long, cold winters, they would spend time with their families and friends, singing along to instruments they had made, telling stories, and playing games.

Bonhomme Carnaval is the mascot of the world's largest winter festival, the Carnaval de Québec.

WHY LEARN FRENCH?

Le Festival du Voyageur

Le Festival du Voyageur is celebrated every year in Winnipeg, Manitoba, usually in February. It honours the voyageurs, who established the first French-speaking communities in western Canada as they travelled across the land, trading with Aboriginal peoples.

Vistors to Le Festival du Voyageur *gather around while stew is prepared over an open fire.*

At Le Festival du Voyageur, La Compagnie de La Vérendrye *reenacts the lives of soldiers who accompanied the Canadian explorer Pierre Gaultier de Varennes, Sieur de La Vérendrye on his quest to explore western Canada between 1725 and 1743.*

Le Carnaval de Québec

Le Carnaval de Québec, often known as *Carnaval,* is celebrated in Quebec City in February. It takes place before the Christian season of Lent, at the same time as Mardi Gras in Louisiana and in Brazil. *Carnaval* is the largest winter festival in the world. Many of you will have seen pictures of the mascot, *Bonhomme Carnaval.* He wears a *ceinture fléchée,* or arrow-patterned sash, around his waist, like the ones that men used to wear around their jackets to keep out the cold.

La Saint-Jean-Baptiste

La Saint-Jean-Baptiste is celebrated on June 24 by French Canadians all over Canada. In 1908, Pope Pius X named Saint John the Baptist the official patron saint of French Canada. French Canadians celebrate their pride and heritage on this day. In Quebec, stores and government offices close and there are large parades and fireworks displays.

Le Congrès mondial acadien

Le Congrès mondial acadien, or Acadian World Congress, celebrates Acadian heritage. Acadians from across North America are invited to the festival. There are concerts, art exhibits, storytelling evenings, picnics, and many family reunions, known as *Les retrouvailles*. The festival takes place every five years around August 15, the official Acadian National Holiday.

Le Festival acadien de Caraquet

Another Acadian festival is *le Festival acadien de Caraquet* in Caraquet, New Brunswick. Every year, for two weeks in August, people celebrate Acadian culture and heritage with music, dance, games, food, poetry readings, and much more.

The highlight of the festival is *le Tintamarre*, which takes place on August 15. Tens of thousands of people gather in the streets and, for one hour, make as much noise as they can with whistles, bells, pots and pans, musical instruments, chainsaws (with the saws removed), and anything else they can think of. The parade marks the expulsion of the Acadians from the region in 1755 after they refused to pledge allegiance to the British crown. Families were torn apart as people were sent to Louisiana and other parts of North America. The noise at *le Tintamarre* is a message to everyone saying, "We, the Acadians, are still here!"

The Acadian flag is blue, white, and red like France's flag, but it also has a yellow star in the blue section. The star represents Mary, the patron saint of Acadians.

Le Tintamarre is celebrated by Acadians everywhere. This photo was taken in Le Pays de la Sagouine, a reproduction of an Acadian village in Bouctouche, New Brunswick.

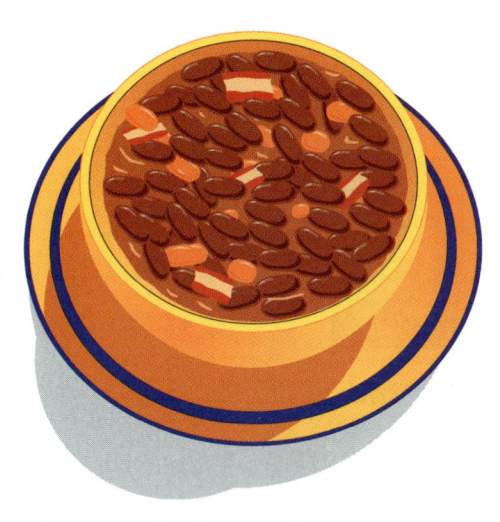

Fèves au lard are often flavoured with maple syrup.

Food

Eating is part of every celebration. People still enjoy many of the same foods that French settlers ate long ago.

- Typical French-Canadian foods, such as *tourtière* (meat pie), *ragoût de boulettes* (meatball stew), *pattes de cochon* (pigs' feet), *soupe aux pois* (pea soup), and *fèves au lard* (baked beans with pork), were made with local ingredients. These heavy meals helped keep loggers and other people who worked outside in the winter warm and well fed.

- Maple trees abound in eastern Canada, and Aboriginal peoples taught the first European settlers how to harvest the sap from the trees to make maple syrup. Did you know that they first ate maple syrup by pouring it on warm bread? Today, as in the past, some French Canadians cook the syrup and spread it on the snow, then roll it up with sticks, such as Popsicle sticks, and eat it. It tastes like delicious, warm taffy. Maple syrup is also poured on pancakes and French toast.

- Crêpes are thin pancakes that were first made in France. They can be rolled up with fruit, ice cream, cheese, chicken, or vegetables inside. You can also top them with your favourite ingredients.

- November 25 is the feast day of Saint Catherine, the patron saint of young girls. On *la fête de la Sainte-Catherine*, French-Canadian families make a tasty treat called *la tire Sainte-Catherine*, or pull taffy. They boil molasses, sugar, and corn syrup, let it cool slightly, then pull and fold the mixture until it becomes a golden colour. Then they wrap the candy in *papillottes*, or small pieces of waxed paper.

- Many cheeses, such as Brie and Camembert, come from France. France has also given us the baguette and made croissants popular. In fact, to this day, a favourite lunch in France is cheese on a baguette.

    Quebec is also famous for its cheeses. Today, Quebec produces more than 300 tasty varieties. One of the best known is Oka. It was first made in 1893 by monks who came from France to live in the village of Oka, near Montreal. They earned a living by making and selling cheese.

- *Poutine* is a French-Canadian dish that is popular across Canada. It is made with French fries, gravy, and cheese curds.

The Arts

The arts have always been an important part of French-Canadian culture. Painters, sculptors, writers, singers, actors, acrobats, and dancers have used their creativity to tell the stories of French Canada, from the time of the original settlers to today.

Here are some famous French-Canadian artists:

- **Céline Dion** has been performing around the world, in both English and French, for many years. She started out singing in French as a young girl with her brothers and sisters and composed her first song with her mother and brother at the age of 12.

- **Gilles Vigneault** is a singer and poet whose songs capture the beauty and heritage of Quebec and its people. One of his most famous songs, "Mon pays," describes his love for his wintry homeland and the people who live there.

- **Calixa Lavallée** composed "O Canada" for the Saint-Jean-Baptiste celebration in 1880 and the poet and judge **Adolphe-Basile Routhier** wrote the original French lyrics. It was more than 20 years later that the first English version of "O Canada" appeared.

O Canada

O Canada ! Terre de nos aïeux,
Ton front est ceint de fleurons glorieux !

Car ton bras sait porter l'épée,
Il sait porter la croix !

Ton histoire est une épopée
Des plus brillants exploits.

Et ta valeur, de foi trempée,
Protégera nos foyers et nos droits.

Protégera nos foyers et nos droits.

- **Marie-Louise Gay** is a children's book illustrator and author whose Grade 3 art teacher failed her on a project because she couldn't draw a symmetrical flower vase. She gave up drawing for a long time, but later decided that she wanted to illustrate and, eventually, write her own stories in both English and French. She has won many awards for her work, including several for her books about Stella, a young girl who introduces her little brother, Sam, to the magical worlds of the forest, sky, sea, and snow.

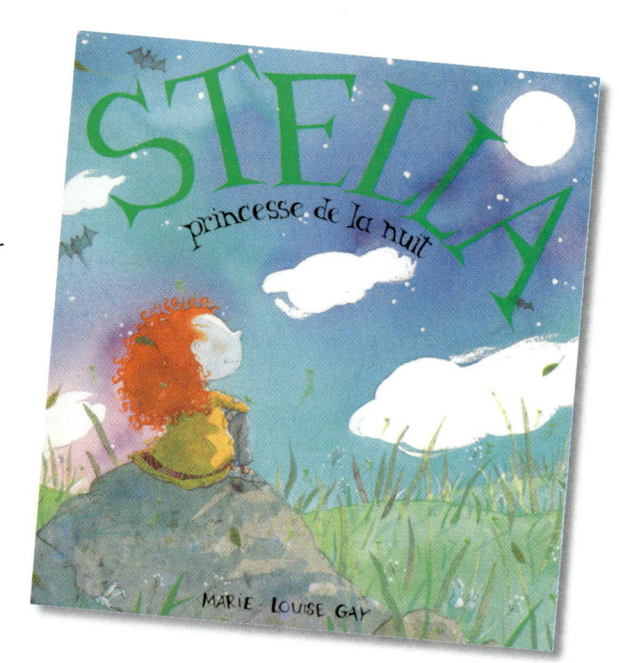

- **Roch Carrier** is a very popular French-Canadian author who wrote the famous story *Le chandail de hockey*, translated as *The Hockey Sweater*. This story tells about a young Montreal Canadiens fan who asks for a new hockey sweater with the number of his favourite player, Maurice "Rocket" Richard, on it. The young boy is shocked when he receives a hockey sweater, but not the one he had hoped for! A quote from the story — in both languages — appears on the back of Canada's $5 bill.

- **Cirque du Soleil** is Canada's world-famous circus. It was created in 1984 by a group of Quebec street performers who wanted to entertain people with spellbinding gymnastics, dramatic acts, original music, and colourful costumes. They balance on eight chairs stacked one on top of another; perform contortionist acts while juggling; dive through hoops; bicycle on high wires; climb up, drop down, jump between, hang from, and spin on top of poles seven metres high; and perform quintuple twisting somersaults with stilts strapped to their legs.

  Today, many different Cirque shows, each one with a different theme, are performed all over the world. One, called O, is performed in, on, and above water.

- **Robert Lepage** is a director, designer, playwright, and actor. He is known for combining different media, including music, dance, filmmaking, video art, and computer graphics, in his work. One of his most complicated projects was The Image Mill, an enormous outdoor architectural projection that celebrated Quebec City's 400th anniversary. Engravings, paintings, photos, and videos that told the story of the city's history were projected onto 81 grain silos measuring 600 metres long and 30 metres high.

Chapter 3
More Famous French Canadians

Many other French Canadians have become well known for their accomplishments in sports, science, law, and many other fields.

- **Jean-Luc Brassard** won the first ever gold medal in freestyle skiing at the 1994 Winter Olympics. In fact, he was the first Canadian to win a gold medal in any snow sport.

  Other well-known French-Canadian athletes are:

  - **Sylvie Fréchette** (synchronized swimming)
  - **Gaétan Boucher** (speed skating)
  - **Guy LaFleur, Maurice "Rocket" Richard, Jacques Plante,** and **Mario Lemieux** (hockey)
  - **Alexandre Despatie** and **Emilie Heymans** (diving)
  - **Gilles Villeneuve** and **Jacques Villeneuve** (racecar driving)

Jean-Luc Brassard started moguls skiing after he became bored with traditional skiing. He won his first World Cup Race when he was 18 years old.

WHY LEARN FRENCH?

- In 1984, **Marc Garneau** became the first Canadian in space. During that flight and two others in 1996 and 2000, he logged more than 677 hours in space. In 2005, he left the Canadian Space Agency to pursue a career in politics. He became a Member of Parliament in 2008.

- **Julie Payette** is another Canadian astronaut. In 1999, she flew on Space Shuttle Discovery, the first mission to dock with the International Space Station. She was responsible for operating the Canadarm. Julie was also chosen as one of the astronauts for Space Shuttle Endeavour's 2009 mission to the International Space Station, to install the remaining parts of an experiment lab built by the Japanese Space Agency.

- **Louise Arbour**, a famous Canadian lawyer, is the former United Nations High Commissioner for Human Rights, a former justice of the Supreme Court of Canada, and a former Chief Prosecutor of war crimes for the International Criminal Tribunals for the former Yugoslavia and Rwanda.

- Before the snowmobile was invented, it was difficult for people living in rural areas of Quebec to travel in winter. **Joseph-Armand Bombardier** was determined to develop a vehicle that could travel on deep snow. He built his first snow machine when he was just 15 years old. It was an unusual-looking sled propelled by a car motor.

  It wasn't until the winter of 1936–37 that Bombardier produced the first snowmobile for sale, the B7. The "B" stood for Bombardier and the "7" stood for the number of passengers it could carry. The first buyers were doctors, ambulance drivers, rural veterinarians, innkeepers, funeral directors, and priests. Before long, transportation, telephone and electricity companies, stores, and letter carriers were using snowmobiles too. Today, many young people in northern Canada go to school by snowmobile.

IT'S A WRAP!

- Look around your home for French words on product labels, on flyers and other brochures, and in books. Try to find at least 10 words. Make a list.
- Look around your town or city. Try to find two signs with French words. What do the signs mean?
- Sing along to a CD of traditional folk songs, such as "Alouette," "V'là l'bon vent," "À la claire fontaine," "Gens du pays," and "Mon merle."

- Early French settlers who played music on their fiddle or accordion were often accompanied by people who played the spoons. Try playing a rhythm using the spoons.

- Make a game of Concentration to play with your family or friends. Include elements of French-Canadian life on your cards, such as foods, festivals, music, athletes, or artists. For example, you can include a person's name on one card and the accomplishment that person is known for on the matching card.

- Do some research on *le bonhomme dansant*. Woodsmen carved this little wooden man with moveable feet and arms. At parties and family gatherings, they would make him "dance" on a wood plank to the sound of fiddle music.

- Research one of the famous French Canadians mentioned here or another famous French Canadian that you're interested in. Tell your friends and family about the person.

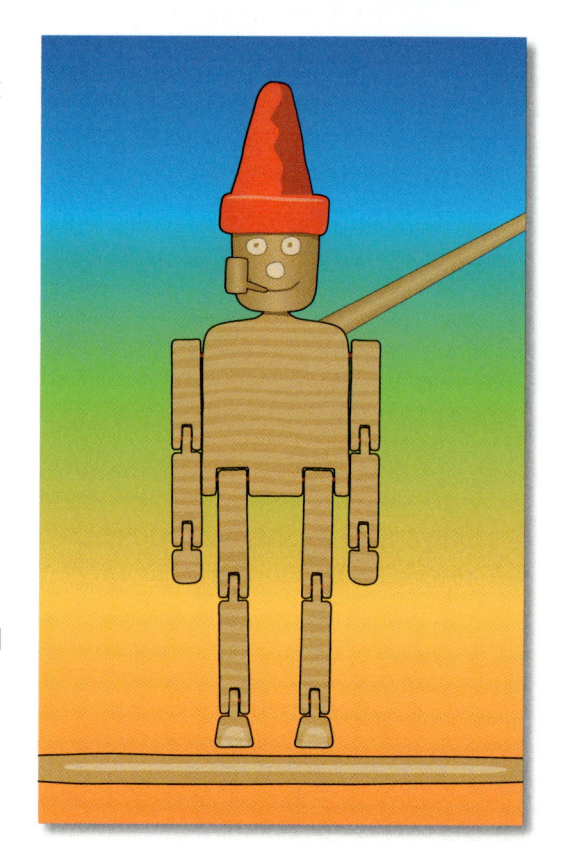

- "Sur le pont d'Avignon" is a song about a bridge in the fortified city of Avignon, in southern France. Teach your friends and family the lyrics and actions that go with it:
  - ▶ Dance in a circle each time you sing the chorus.
  - ▶ As you sing the first verse, stop dancing while the boys bow ("*font comme ça*") and pretend to raise their hats ("*et puis encore comme ça*").
  - ▶ As you sing the second verse, stop dancing while the girls curtsy to one side ("*font comme ça*") and then to the other side ("*et puis encore comme ça*").

  Make up additional verses and actions if you like.

Sur le pont d'Avignon

Refrain

Sur le pont d'Avignon
On y danse, on y danse,
Sur le pont d'Avignon
On y danse tout en rond.

Les beaux messieurs font comme ça
Et puis encore comme ça.

Refrain

Les belles dames font comme ça
Et puis encore comme ça.

Refrain

On the Bridge of Avignon

Chorus

On the bridge of Avignon
They are dancing, they are dancing,
On the bridge of Avignon
They are dancing round and round.

The handsome gentlemen do like this
And then they do like that.

Chorus

The pretty ladies do like this
And then they do like that.

Chorus

Le pont d'Avignon, also known as le pont Saint-Bénézet, was built between 1177 and 1185. Originally 920 metres long and 4 metres wide, with 22 arches, it was partially destroyed by battles and floods. Today, only four of the original arches remain.

WHY LEARN FRENCH?

ADULTS CAN HELP

- To help your child appreciate and enjoy French-Canadian culture, plan a French-Canadian day at home. Serve traditional French-Canadian foods and watch a French TV program or DVD together.

- If there is a story in the newspaper or on TV about a French Canadian's accomplishments, talk about it with your child so that he or she begins to realize the contributions that French Canadians make to our country.

- If possible, take part in a French event in your community or another region of Canada — for example, a festival, concert, or visit to a French bookstore or restaurant. Encourage your child to speak French as much as possible as you order food, purchase tickets, or participate in activities. Model this for your child by speaking as much French as you can.

Part 2: The Letter

Chapter 1: Letters and Sounds

The Alphabet

French uses the same 26-letter alphabet as English, and as in English, the letters are divided into consonants and vowels.

Consonants

b, c, d, f, g, h, j, k, l, m, n, p, q, r, s, t, v, w, x, y, z

Vowels

a, e, i, o, u, and sometimes y

The French alphabet may look the same as the English alphabet, but the names of the letters are pronounced differently. Some of the letters are pronounced differently too.

The chart on page 24 shows the approximate French pronunciation for the name of each letter. Your French teacher will help you pronounce each sound.

Y can be either a consonant or a vowel, just as in English.

Consonant

le yoghurt

le yoyo

Vowel

le gymnase

la bicyclette

LETTER	APPROXIMATE PRONUNCIATION OF THE NAME OF THE LETTER	LETTER	APPROXIMATE PRONUNCIATION OF THE NAME OF THE LETTER
A	ah (as in "f**a**ther")	N	en
B	bay	O	oh
C	say	P	pay
D	day	Q	kew
E	euh (as in "b**oo**k")	R	ehr
F	ef	S	es
G	zhay	T	tay
H	ash	U	ew
I	ee	V	vay
J	jhee	W	doo-bleuh-vay
K	ka (as in "**ca**t")	X	eeks
L	el	Y	ee-grek
M	em	Z	zed

TRY THIS!
Spell your name out loud.

French Accents

Unlike in English, French vowels are frequently written with accents. Some vowels sound the same with and without an accent or with different accents; other vowels sound different. (See the Pronunciation Guide on pages 81–83 for information on how to pronounce many French sounds.)

Many of the accents come from Old French. Often they were added to replace other letters. Some books treated these accented vowels as additional vowels, which would have made the French alphabet 36 letters long!

WHAT THE ACCENT IS CALLED	WHERE YOU MIGHT SEE THE ACCENT	WHAT THE LETTER SOUNDS LIKE WITH THE ACCENT (APPROXIMATE)
l'accent aigu	é	"ay" in w**ay**
l'accent grave	à	"a" in c**a**t
	è	"e" in l**e**t
	ù	"ew" in gr**ew**
l'accent circonflexe	â	"a" in f**a**ther
	ê	"e" in l**e**t
	î	"ee" in str**ee**t
	ô	"o" in b**oa**t
	û	"ew" in gr**ew**
le tréma	ë	"e" in l**e**t
	ï	"ee" in str**ee**t
	ü	"ew" in gr**ew**
la cédille	ç	"s" in **S**unday

Adding an accent sometimes changes the meaning of a word.

ou (or)
où (where)

âge (age)
âgé (old)

TRY THIS!

Use what you know about accents and check out the Pronunciation Guide on pages 81–83 to read these words out loud:

- le père
- le bébé
- français

le père, le bébé

THE LETTER

25

Special Letter Combinations

Certain French sounds are made up of two or more letters that are pronounced together. The letters can be two vowels, two consonants, or a vowel and a consonant.

Some Common Letter Combinations

SPELLING	APPROXIMATE ENGLISH PRONUNCIATION	SAMPLE FRENCH WORDS
er, ez, ai	"ay" in w**ay**	jou**er**, mont**ez**, **ai**mer
ai	"e" in l**e**t	l**ai**t
au, eau	"o" in n**o**se	s**au**ce, **eau**
ou	"oo" in r**oo**m	gen**ou**
eu, eux	"oo" in b**oo**k	h**eu**r**eux**
oui	"wee" in **wee**d	**oui**
gn	"ny" in ca**ny**on	oi**gn**on
oi	"wha" in **wha**t	tr**oi**s

le lait

The following letter combinations all have a nasal sound. Hold your nose to practise saying each sound. Don't pronounce the consonant at the end of the letter combination; it doesn't have its own sound.

SPELLING	APPROXIMATE ENGLISH PRONUNCIATION	SAMPLE FRENCH WORDS
in, im, aim, en	"e" in **e**nter	mat**in**, **im**possible, f**aim**, europé**en**
an, en, em	"a" in w**a**nt	d**an**se, mom**en**t, t**em**ps
on, om	"o" in ph**o**ne	l**on**g, p**om**pe
un, um	"u" in s**u**n	**un**, parf**um**

le parfum

If two vowels are supposed to be pronounced separately, they are written with a tréma: **Noël – pronounced like no-el**.

TRY THIS!
Say these words out loud:
- Joyeux Noël !
- un moment
- deux genoux

Special Consonants

- The letter H is pronounced so lightly that you can barely hear it.
- A double S between two vowels is pronounced like an S.

      assiette

A single S between two vowels is pronounced like a Z.

      oiseau

If the single S is not between two vowels, then it is pronounced like an S.

      histoire

- The letter R is fun to pronounce in French because it comes from the back of your throat. Pretend you're gargling, and do it for a few seconds. That's what the R should sound like.
- C is pronounced like a K when it's followed by an A, O, or U.

      carte

C sounds like an S when it's followed by an E, I, or Y.

      cinéma

To make the C sound like an S in front of an A, O, or U, we add a *cédille*.

      François

- G is pronounced like a hard G when it's followed by an A, O, or U.

      garage

G sounds like a soft G when it's followed by an E, I, or Y.

      garage

To soften the G when it's in front of an A, O, or U, we add an E after the G.

      mangeons

THE LETTER

TRY THIS!

Try these tongue twisters. Use the Pronunciation Guide on pages 81–83 to help you.

- Lise laisse ses chaussettes sécher.
  (Lise lets her socks dry.)

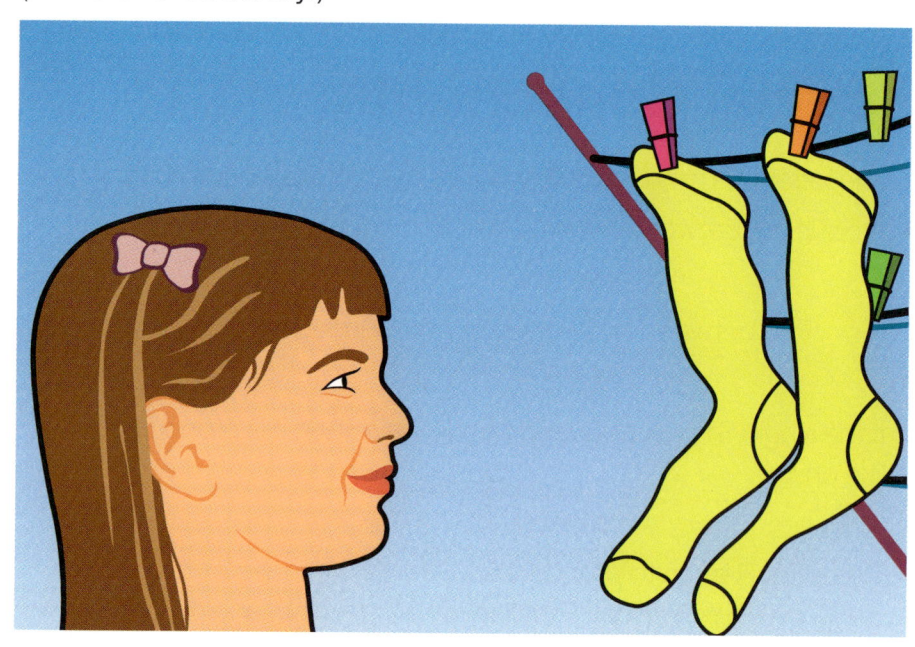

- Roger attrape trois grands rats.
  (Roger catches three big rats.)

Pronouncing Final Consonants

If the last letter of a word is a consonant, it is not pronounced unless:

- the first letter of the next word is a vowel.

  tout à coup

  If the word TOUT were by itself, how would it be pronounced?

- the consonant is a C, R, F, or L. These four consonants are pronounced even if they are at the end of a word. To remember this, think of the word **CAREFUL**, which has the same four consonants.

  Shediac

  erreur

  chef

  nouvel

If the last **two** letters of a word are consonants, neither one is pronounced. For example, neither the P nor the S is pronounced in *temps*.

temps

TRY THIS!

Pronounce these words. Remember the rules for pronouncing final consonants. Use the Pronunciation Guide on pages 81–83 to help you.

- complet
- anglais
- heureux
- un grand arbre

complète
anglaise
heureuse
un petit arbre

un grand arbre   un petit arbre

IT'S A WRAP!

Now that you know some of the pronunciation rules, practise saying these words. Use the Pronunciation Guide on pages 81–83 to help you.

possible	chef
école	complet
petit	heureux
français	française
non	oncle
haricot	oui
chaîne	sauter
année	wagon
passé	assez
qui	chapeau
longtemps	patin

ADULTS CAN HELP

- Practise French pronunciation with your child on a regular basis. Generally, when students begin learning French they enjoy mimicking the sounds, but as they get older they become more self-conscious and often revert to an English pronunciation. Help them become confident in their ability to pronounce French words. Show them that you are not afraid to try to pronounce new French words.

- If your child is writing sentences or small paragraphs, check to see if the words that need accents are spelled correctly. You might ask your child: "What words need accents? Did you put them all in correctly?"

Part 3: Parts of Speech

Chapter 1 — Nouns (Les noms)

Common and Proper Nouns

Common nouns (*noms communs*) are general names for people, places, and things.

sac à dos, fleur, maison, centre commercial, école, stylo

Days of the week are common nouns. Unlike in English, they are not capitalized. When we list them in French, we always start with Monday.

lundi, mardi, mercredi, jeudi, vendredi, samedi, dimanche

Months of the year are also common nouns that are not capitalized in French.

janvier, février, mars, avril, mai, juin, juillet, août, septembre, octobre, novembre, décembre

Proper nouns (*noms propres*) are names of specific people, places, and things. In English, proper nouns always begin with a capital letter. In French, most proper nouns begin with a capital letter, but a few don't.

Sébastien, Annie, madame Thériault, le Canadien, l'Américaine, Noël, monsieur Hébert, France, Ottawa, Nouveau-Brunswick

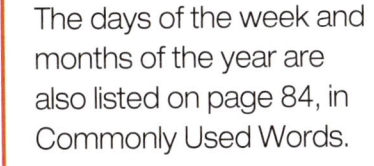

> The days of the week and months of the year are also listed on page 84, in Commonly Used Words.

septembre

lundi	mardi	mercredi	jeudi	vendredi	samedi	dimanche
1	2	3	4	5	6	7
8	9	10	11	12	13	14
15	16	17	18	19	20	21
22	23	24	25	26	27	28
29	30					

Masculine and Feminine Nouns

Unlike English, French nouns are either **masculine** or **feminine**. When you see French written or hear it spoken, you'll notice a small word such as LE or LA in front of every noun. LE tells you the noun is masculine. LA tells you the noun is feminine.

If a noun begins with a vowel or with an H, LE or LA becomes L'. When this happens, you can't use LE or LA to tell whether the noun is masculine or feminine.

le arbre → **l'arbre**

la horloge → **l'horloge**

When you learn a noun, always learn it with LE or LA in front of it. That's the way French children learn the gender.

la chaise

le garçon

le livre

le pupitre

Determiners

The small words that come before nouns are called **determiners**. French nouns are always preceded by a determiner.

Definite Articles

- LE, LA, and LES are special kinds of determiners called **definite articles**. They all mean "the" and they tell you whether a noun is masculine, feminine, or plural.

le chapeau, la chaise, les bébés

Indefinite Articles

- UN, UNE, and DES are special kinds of determiners called **indefinite articles**. They mean "a" or "some," depending on whether the noun is masculine (un), feminine (une), or plural (des).

un chien, une bicyclette, des livres

Partitive Articles

- Sometimes instead of using UN, UNE, or DES to say "some," we use DU, DE LA, DE L', or DES. These are called **partitive articles**; that means that they are a part of a whole thing. They are always found in front of a noun.

Je mange des bonbons.	→	I eat (some) candy.
Tu fais du travail.	→	You do (some) work.
Je bois du lait au déjeuner.	→	I drink (some) milk at breakfast.
Je prends de la réglisse rouge.	→	I take (some) red licorice.

Numbers

- You can also use numbers in front of nouns. If you use numbers, you don't need to use LE, LA, LES, UN, UNE, DU, DE LA, DE L', or DES. See page 92, in Commonly Used Words, for numbers from 0 to 100.

trois hommes, cinq enfants

quatre femmes

PARTS OF SPEECH

How Do You Know If a Noun Is Masculine or Feminine?

- Many common nouns for people have a masculine and feminine form. The two forms are spelled slightly differently: the feminine forms end with an E, and there can be other small variations (a doubled consonant, for example).

MASCULINE	FEMININE	ENGLISH
l'ami	l'amie	friend
le cousin	la cousine	cousin
l'enseignant	l'enseignante	teacher
l'Anglais	l'Anglaise	Englishman/woman
le champion	la championne	champion

- Some common nouns for animals also have a masculine and feminine form. Sometimes, the names of the animals are completely different for males and females.

MASCULINE	FEMININE	ENGLISH
un chat	une chatte	cat
un chien	une chienne	dog
un ours	une ourse	bear
un taureau	une vache	bull/cow
un coq	une poule	rooster/hen

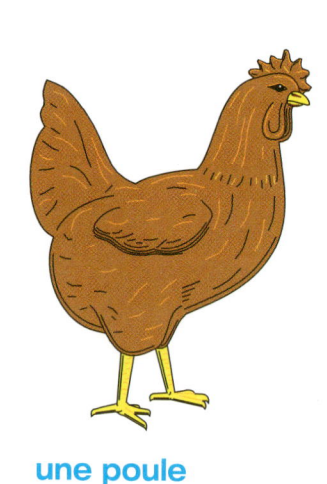

un coq

une poule

- Some nouns are the same whether they're referring to a male or female.

FRENCH	ENGLISH	FRENCH	ENGLISH
adulte	adult	dentiste	dentist
artiste	artist	élève	student
astronaute	astronaut	enfant	child
concierge	caretaker	pilote	pilot
cycliste	cyclist	vétérinaire	veterinarian

- The days of the week, months of the year, and seasons are always masculine.

le lundi, le novembre, le printemps

If you see a noun and you're not sure whether it's masculine or feminine, check in the French section of a French-English dictionary. After the noun, you'll see *n. m.* for *nom masculin* or *n. f.* for *nom féminin*. If you see just *n.*, it means that the noun can be masculine or feminine, depending on whether it relates to a male or a female.

dragon *n. m.* Un dragon est un animal imaginaire. Il a des ailes et une longue queue et il crache du feu.

TRY THIS!

- Look at the lists of nouns for people and animals in the first two charts on page 34. Most of the nouns are pronounced differently depending on whether they are masculine or feminine. Two of them are pronounced the same way in both forms. What are they? (Hint: Use what you learned about pronouncing consonants and letter combinations in Part 2, as well as the Pronunciation Guide on pages 81–83.)

- Decide whether the following words are masculine or feminine. Put LE, LA, or L' in front of them to show your answer. If you're not sure, check a French or French-English dictionary. You'll probably remember some of these from your French class.

porte	classe
bébé	frère
dame	monsieur
mercredi	Ontario
tableau	ordinateur
maman	papa
astronaute	pomme
sœur	tante
printemps	vache

Check your answers using Appendix 2: Answer Key.

la chaise

les chaises

Singular and Plural Nouns

Singular nouns name only one person, place, or thing. Plural nouns name more than one person, place, or thing.

Usually, we add an S to the end of a noun to make it plural. We also use LES in front of a noun instead of LE or LA when it's plural.

la vidéo	→	les vidéos
l'amie	→	les amies
le sac à dos	→	les sacs à dos

Here are some exceptions to the rule:

- We add an X to nouns that end in EU, EAU, or OU to make them plural.

le jeu	→	les jeux
le tableau	→	les tableaux
le genou	→	les genoux

- We change some nouns ending in AL to AUX to make them plural.

| le journal | → | les journaux |
| l'animal | → | les animaux |

- Some nouns don't change in the plural.

Nouns that already end in an S or a Z don't change.

| le pois | → | les pois |
| le nez | → | les nez |

Family names also don't change.

Les Tremblay

TRY THIS!

Change these singular nouns to plural nouns.

- la pomme → les _____
- le cheval → les _____
- un chou → des _____
- le menton → les _____
- la main → les _____
- le morceau → les _____
- le neveu → les _____
- le métal → les _____
- un Irlandais → des _____
- le gaz → les _____
- un Français → des _____
- la famille Bélanger → les _____

Check your answers using Appendix 2: Answer Key.

Pronouns (Les pronoms)

Pronouns are words that are used to replace a noun. Generally, they are used to avoid repeating the noun. Pronouns are masculine or feminine, depending on the noun they replace.

Subject Pronouns

Subject pronouns are used to identify the person or thing doing the action.

FRENCH	ENGLISH
je	I
tu	you (singular, familiar)
il	he
elle	she
nous	we
vous	you (singular, formal; plural)
ils	they (masculine)
elles	they (feminine)

Caroline parle. → Elle parle.
Samantha et Marc jouent à la balle. → Ils jouent à la balle.

Elle lance la balle.

Je

JE becomes J' before a vowel or a silent H.

Je marche vite.
J'aime lire.
J'habite à Calgary

TU and VOUS

There are two ways to say "you" in French: TU and VOUS. Use TU when you're speaking to a younger child, a friend, a relative, or someone else you know well. Use VOUS in a more formal situation — for example, when you're speaking to a person you don't know well or someone to whom you should show respect. Also use VOUS when you're speaking to more than one person.

ILS and ELLES

Use ILS when you're talking about a group of all boys (or masculine objects) or a mixed group of boys and girls (or masculine and feminine objects). Use ELLES when you're talking about a group of all girls (or all feminine objects).

TRY THIS!

Replace the underlined term with the correct subject pronoun.

- Marc et Paul jouent dans le parc. _____ jouent dans le parc.
- Hélène parle à son ami. _____ parle à son ami.
- Julie et Sophia regardent un film. _____ regardent un film.
- Joshua et Natalie mangent le petit déjeuner. _____ mangent le petit déjeuner.
- Daniel court vite. _____ court vite.

Check your answers using Appendix 2: Answer Key.

Adjectives (Les adjectifs)

Chapter 3

An adjective is a word that describes a noun or pronoun.

un grand problème
une petite fille
une pomme rouge
une cycliste canadienne

une pomme rouge

Masculine and Feminine Adjectives

To describe a masculine noun, the adjective must be masculine. To describe a feminine noun, the adjective must be feminine. Here's the most common way to make masculine adjectives feminine:

Step 1: Look at the end of the adjective.
Step 2: Add an E to the masculine form.

| grand | → | grande |
| petit | → | petite |

If the masculine adjective already ends in an E, there is no change for the feminine.

| calme | → | calme |
| triste | → | triste |

Singular and Plural Adjectives

To describe a plural noun, the adjective must be plural. The most common way to make an adjective plural is to add an S to the masculine or feminine form of the adjective.

| le grand garçon | → | les grands garçons |
| la fille heureuse | → | les filles heureuses |

TRY THIS!

Make the adjectives in brackets agree with the nouns they modify. Note: The adjectives may be correct as they are.

- une (petit) maison
- une dame (triste)
- la porte (ouvert)
- un (grand) garçon
- les chandails (rouge)
- les (grand) écoles

Check your answers using Appendix 2: Answer Key.

Possessive Adjectives (Les adjectifs possessifs)

Possessive adjectives show to whom a thing or person belongs; for example, MY dog, YOUR friends, or HER family.

A possessive adjective that describes a feminine noun (thing or person) must be feminine. A possessive adjective that describes a masculine noun must be masculine. A possessive adjective that describes a plural noun must be plural. Remember: It doesn't matter to whom the object belongs. What matters is whether the noun is masculine or feminine.

Voici ma mère.

Voici mon père.

Voici mes parents.

MASCULINE NOUN (SINGULAR)	FEMININE NOUN (SINGULAR)	PLURAL NOUNS (MASCULINE AND FEMININE)	ENGLISH
mon	ma	mes	my
ton	ta	tes	your (singular, familiar)
son	sa	ses	his, her, or its
notre	notre	nos	our
votre	votre	vos	your (singular, formal; plural)
leur	leur	leurs	their

PARTS OF SPEECH

We can also use the French preposition DE to show possession. It is used in front of a noun or a name (where in English we would use 'S or S' after the noun or name).

FORM OF DE	WHEN TO USE IT	EXAMPLE	ENGLISH
de	before the name of a person or place	C'est la mère **de** Paul.	That's Paul's mother.
du	before a masculine noun	C'est la patte **du** chien.	That's the dog's paw.
de la	before a feminine noun	C'est la maison **de la** famille Dubuc.	That's the Dubuc family's home.
de l'	before a noun that begins with a vowel or a silent H	C'est le chapeau **de l'**homme.	That's the man's hat.
des	before a plural noun (masculine or feminine)	C'est la balle **des** enfants.	That's the children's ball.

For more information on prepositions, see page 54.

TRY THIS!

How would you say each of these?

- my uncle (un oncle)
- Nicole's sisters (une sœur)
- his hockey stick (un bâton de hockey)
- the girl's book (le livre)
- your friends (des amis)
- the children's ball (la balle)
- her skates (les patins)
- our mother (la mère)
- their boots (les bottes)
- the elephant's tail (la queue)
- the baby's toy (le jouet)

Check your answers using Appendix 2: Answer Key.

Interrogative Adjectives (Les adjectifs interrogatifs)

Interrogative adjectives are adjectives that are used to ask a question. Like other adjectives, they show whether a noun is masculine or feminine, singular or plural.

Here are the interrogative adjectives:

INTERROGATIVE ADJECTIVE	FORM	EXAMPLE	ENGLISH
Quel	masculine, singular	Quel arbre ?	Which tree?
Quelle	feminine, singular	Quelle pomme ?	Which apple?
Quels	masculine or mixed, plural	Quels garcons ?	Which boys?
Quelles	feminine, plural	Quelles filles ?	Which girls?

QUELS and QUELLES

Use QUELS when you're asking about a group of all boys (or masculine objects) or a mixed group of boys and girls (or masculine and feminine objects). Use QUELLES when you're asking about a group of all girls (or feminine objects).

Placement of Adjectives

Most adjectives are placed after the noun they describe.

une voiture rouge – a red car
un livre noir – a black book
une femme canadienne – a Canadian woman
une église catholique – a Catholic church
une histoire intéressante – an interesting story

Possessive and interrogative adjectives are placed in front of the noun.

mon enfant – my child
Quel stylo ? – Which pen?

Here are some other adjectives that come before the noun.

une jeune fille
une vieux bateau
un nouveau livre
une jolie fleur
une grosse citrouille
une longue distance
un bon film
un mauvais rêve
un grand parapluie
un petit bébé
un beau garçon
une haute montagne

Chapter 4: Verbs

A verb is the main part of speech in a sentence. Most verbs describe an action.

Je mange une pomme.
Tu parles à ton frère.
Elle joue au baseball.

Some verbs describe a state of being.

Nous sommes heureux.
J'ai mal à la tête.

See pages 93–94, in Commonly Used Words, for lists of verbs.

Elle joue au baseball.

ER, IR, and RE Verbs

In English, the infinitive form of a verb includes the word "to": to read, to jump, to smile.

In French, verbs are divided into categories depending on whether the infinitive ends in ER, IR, or RE.

ER Verbs

Most verbs end in ER in their infinitive form.

aimer (to like)
parler (to speak)
écouter (to listen)
jouer (to play)

We change the endings of verbs to show who is doing the action, or who the subject of the sentence is. Each verb tense (for example, present, past, or future) has different endings. The present tense is the one most students learn first.

Here's how to add endings for the present tense of ER verbs:

Step 1: Find the root of the verb by removing the ER from the infinitive.

aim   er

Step 2: Add these endings to the root:

je	→	e
tu	→	es
il	→	e
elle	→	e
nous	→	ons
vous	→	ez
ils	→	ent
elles	→	ent

Here's what the verb AIMER looks like with different endings:

J'aime les animaux. (I like animals)
Tu aimes les animaux.
Il aime les animaux.
Elle aime les animaux.
Nous aimons les animaux.
Vous aimez les animaux.
Ils aiment les animaux.
Elles aiment les animaux.

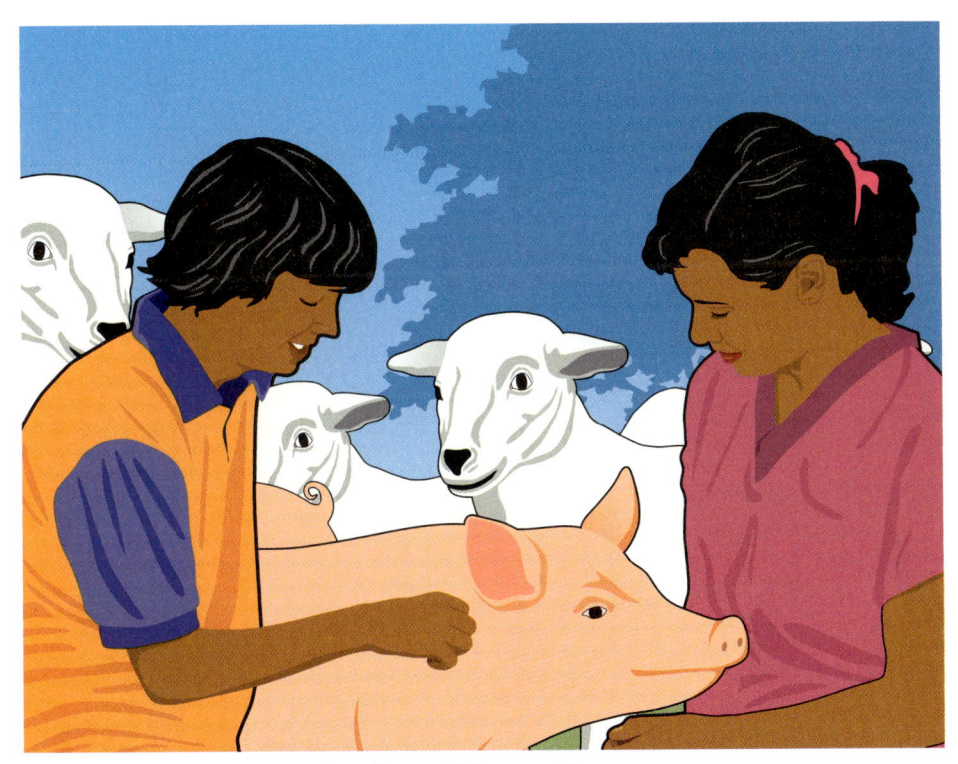

Ils aiment les animaux.

PARTS OF SPEECH

IR Verbs

Some verbs end in IR in their infinitive form.

finir (to finish)
choisir (to choose)

Here's how to add endings for the present tense of IR verbs:

Step 1: Find the root of the verb by removing the IR from the infinitive.

fin**ir**

Step 2: Add these endings to the root.

je	→	is
tu	→	is
il	→	it
elle	→	it
nous	→	issons
vous	→	issez
ils	→	issent
elles	→	issent

Here's what the verb FINIR looks like with different endings:

Je finis mes devoirs. (I finish my homework.)
Tu finis tes devoirs.
Il finit ses devoirs.
Elle finit ses devoirs.
Nous finissons nos devoirs.
Vous finissez vos devoirs.
Ils finissent leurs devoirs.
Elles finissent leurs devoirs.

RE Verbs

Some verbs end in RE in their infinitive form.

attendre (to wait)
entendre (to hear)
répondre (to answer)

Here's how to add endings for the present tense of RE verbs:

Step 1: Find the root of the verb by removing the RE from the infinitive.

attend**re**

Step 2: Add these endings to the root.

je	→	s
tu	→	s
il	→	(nothing)
elle	→	(nothing)
nous	→	ons
vous	→	ez
ils	→	ent
elles	→	ent

Here's what the verb ATTENDRE looks like with different endings:

J'attends l'autobus. (I wait for the bus.)
Tu attends l'autobus.
Il attend l'autobus.
Elle attend l'autobus.
Nous attendons l'autobus.
Vous attendez l'autobus.
Ils attendent l'autobus.
Elles attendent l'autobus.

Elle attend l'autobus.

PARTS OF SPEECH

Check your answers using Appendix 2: Answer Key.

TRY THIS!
How would you say the following?
- We talk. (nous, parler)
- You choose. (tu, choisir)
- I run. (je, courir)
- They hear the dog. (ils, entendre le chien)
- You wait for your turn. (vous, attendre votre tour)
- She plays the piano. (elle, jouer du piano)

Common Irregular Verbs

Some verbs are irregular. This means that they do not follow the same patterns as other verbs in their group.

Four very common irregular verbs are AVOIR (to have), ÊTRE (to be), ALLER (to go), and FAIRE (to make). They do not follow the pattern for ER, IR, and RE verbs. They are used often and their root changes, so it's a good idea to memorize them.

AVOIR
J'ai deux frères.
Tu as deux frères.
Il a deux frères.
Elle a deux frères.
Nous avons deux frères.
Vous avez deux frères.
Ils ont deux frères.
Elles ont deux frères.

ÊTRE
Je suis canadien.
Tu es canadien.
Il est canadien.
Elle est canadienne.
Nous sommes canadiens.
Vous êtes canadiens.
Ils sont canadiens.
Elles sont canadiens.

ALLER
Je vais à l'école.
Tu vas à l'école.
Il va à l'école.
Elle va à l'école.
Nous allons à l'école.
Vous allez à l'école.
Ils vont à l'école.
Elles vont à l'école.

FAIRE
Je fais un bonhomme de neige.
Tu fais un bonhomme de neige.
Il fait un bonhomme de neige.
Elle fait un bonhomme de neige.
Nous faisons un bonhomme de neige.
Vous faites un bonhomme de neige.
Ils font un bonhomme de neige.
Elles font un bonhomme de neige.

Ils font un bonhomme de neige.

PARTS OF SPEECH

Check your answers using Appendix 2: Answer Key.

TRY THIS!

Choose one of the irregular verbs on pages 48–49 to complete each sentence. Use the correct form of the verb. Say the sentence out loud.

- Elle _____ intelligente.
- Nous _____ un gâteau.
- Vous _____ à la bibliothèque.
- Il _____ douze ans.

Expressions with AVOIR and FAIRE

The verbs AVOIR and FAIRE are used in many expressions. Here are some examples:

J'ai froid. (I'm cold.)

J'ai chaud. (I'm hot.)

J'ai faim. (I'm hungry.)

J'ai soif. (I'm thirsty.)

J'ai mal à la tête. (I have a headache.)

J'ai 12 ans. (I'm 12 years old.)

J'ai besoin de . . . (I need . . .)

Il fait froid. (It's cold.)

Il fait chaud. (It's hot.)

Il fait beau. (It's nice out.)

Je fais mes devoirs. (I do my homework.)

Je fais attention. (I'm paying attention.)

Je fais du sport. (I play sports.)

The Imperative (L'impératif)

The imperative is the form of the verb that gives commands. It is easy to learn and use. To form the imperative, simply use the TU, NOUS, and VOUS forms of the present tense of the verb you need.

There are two small things to remember:

- You must take the "s" off the TU form of the verb when you write the imperative.
- In English, whenever you see the word "let's," this means you use the imperative "nous" form in French.

LE PRÉSENT	L'IMPÉRATIF
Tu **vas** à la fenêtre. (You go to the window.)	**Va** à la fenêtre. (Go to the window.)
Tu **manges** ton souper. (You eat your supper.)	**Mange** ton souper. (Eat your supper.)
Nous **étudions** ce soir. (We're studying tonight.)	**Étudions** ce soir. (Let's study tonight.)
Nous **parlons** français dans la salle de classe. (We speak French in class.)	**Parlons** français dans la salle de classe. (Let's speak French in class.)
Vous **allez** au cinéma samedi. (You're going to the movies on Saturday.)	**Allez** au cinéma samedi. (Go to the movies on Saturday.)

TRY THIS!

Change these sentences from the present tense to the imperative.

- Nous chantons une chanson.
- Tu manges tes légumes.
- Vous écoutez bien.

Check your answers using Appendix 2: Answer Key.

PARTS OF SPEECH

Chapter 5: Adverbs

Types of Adverbs

Adverbs describe verbs, adjectives, or other adverbs. Some adverbs tell how something happened.

Nous courons vite. (We run quickly.)
Tu manges lentement. (You eat slowly.)
Vous dansez bien. (You dance well.)
Ils chantent mal. (They sing poorly.)
Elle parle poliment. (She speaks politely.)

Some adverbs describe how many or how much.

J'ai assez de pommes. (I have enough apples.)
Vous avez peu de raisins. (You have few grapes.)
Guillaume a trop de bonbons. (Guillaume has too many candies.)
Nous avons beaucoup de devoirs. (We have a lot of homework.)
Je suis très fatigué. (I am very tired.)
Elle regarde souvent la télévision. (She often watches television.)
Ils visitent rarement leur grand-mère. (They seldom visit their grandmother.)

Guillaume a trop de bonbons.

TRY THIS!

Insert an adverb that makes sense. Choose from the adverbs on page 52.

- Jean donne des bonbons à tous ses amis. Il a _____ de bonbons.
- Maman a quatre biscuits. Il y a cinq enfants. Maman n'a pas _____ biscuits.
- Simon n'aime pas le dentiste. Il marche _____ pour aller chez le dentiste.
- C'est la récréation. Les élèves vont _____ dans la cour d'école.
- Marie joue _____ au volleyball, mais elle joue _____ du piano. Elle n'est pas bonne musicienne.

Check your answers using Appendix 2: Answer Key.

Chapter 6: Small But Important Words

Nouns, verbs, adjectives, and adverbs are key parts of a sentence, but there are other types of words that help you say what you mean. These words are often small, but they're important.

Prepositions (Les prépositions)

A preposition usually tells where or when. Here are some common prepositions:

PREPOSITION	EXAMPLE
après (after)	Elle entre **après** Marie. (She enters after Marie.)
avec (with)	Je travaille **avec** ma sœur. (I work with my sister.)
dans (in)	Mets ton cahier **dans** la boîte. (Put your workbook in the box.)
entre (between)	Deux est **entre** un et trois. (Two is between one and three.)
pour (for)	Ce cadeau est **pour** Jacques. (This present is for Jacques.)
de (from)	Je suis **de** Moncton. (I'm from Moncton.)

You'll find more prepositions on page 95, in Commonly Used Words.

Deux est entre un et trois.

Conjunctions (Les conjonctions)

Conjunctions are like bridges that join words, phrases, clauses, and sentences. Here are some common conjunctions:

CONJUNCTION	EXAMPLE
et (and)	Panos **et** William jouent au baseball dans la cour. (Panos and William are playing baseball in the yard.)
mais (but)	J'aime nager **mais** je n'aime pas patiner. (I like swimming but I don't like skating.)
ou (or)	Est-ce que tu veux manger de la pizza **ou** un hamburger ? (Do you want to eat pizza or a hamburger?)
parce que (because)	Je porte mon manteau **parce qu'**il fait froid dehors. (I'm wearing my coat because it's cold outside.)
quand (when)	Elle reste à la maison **quand** elle est malade. (She stays home when she's sick.)

Interjections (Les interjections)

Interjections are words, phrases, and nonsense words that express strong feelings. Interjections are usually punctuated with exclamation points.

Here are some common interjections:

- Miam ! Miam ! (Mmm! Good!)
- D'accord. (OK.)
- Hein ? (Eh?)
- Désolé ! (Sorry!)
- Allô ! (Hi!)

In French, unlike in English, there's a space before exclamation marks, question marks, colons, and semi-colons. There's no space before periods or commas.

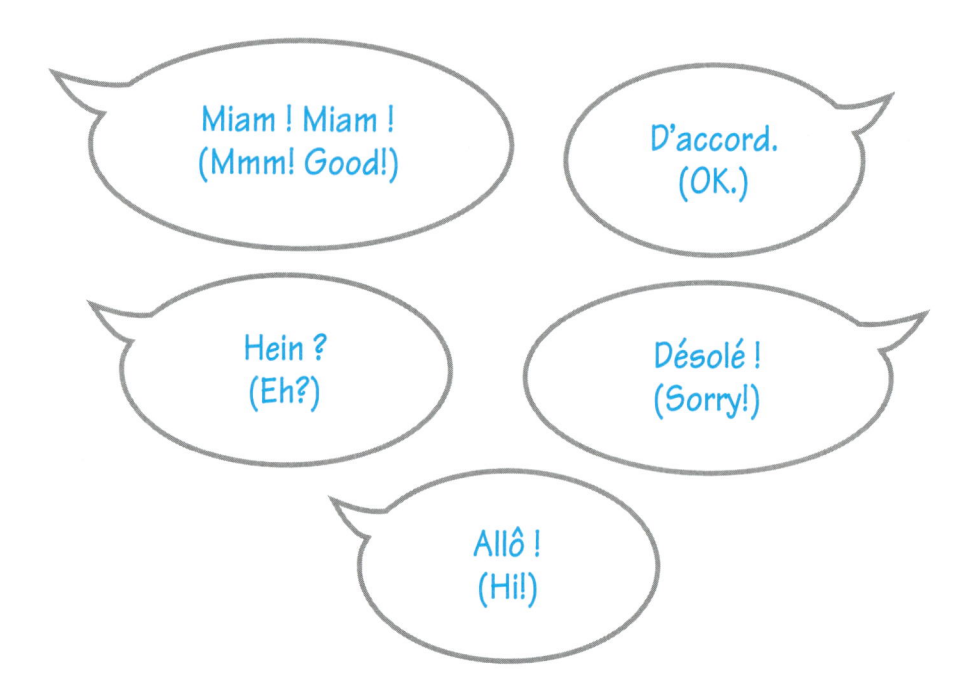

You'll find more interjections on page 95, in Commonly Used Words.

TRY THIS!

Choose one of the prepositions, conjunctions, or interjections you learned to complete each sentence.

- _____ ! C'est délicieux !
- Julie _____ Thomas mangent des biscuits.
- J'aime le baseball _____ je n'aime pas le soccer.
- Marc va au cinéma _____ son père.
- Voilà un livre _____ Manon.

Check your answers using Appendix 2: Answer Key.

Chapter 7: Putting It All Together

The Sentence

As in English, French words work together in very specific ways to form sentences. Each word in a sentence has an important role to play.

A sentence is made up of at least a subject and a verb. Most sentences also have an object after the verb.

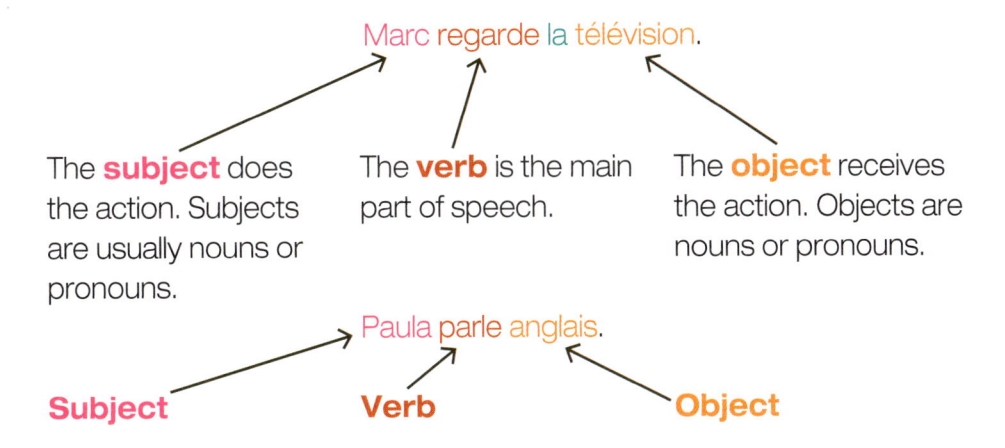

Marc regarde la télévision.

The **subject** does the action. Subjects are usually nouns or pronouns.

The **verb** is the main part of speech.

The **object** receives the action. Objects are nouns or pronouns.

Paula parle anglais.

Subject   **Verb**   **Object**

Making a Sentence Negative

To make a sentence negative, you need two words. The most common words are NE and PAS, which together mean "not." NE comes before the verb and PAS comes after.

Je marche. (I walk.)
Je ne marche pas. (I do not walk.)

Lucien

ne
mange
pas.

Think of a hamburger when you make a sentence negative. NE is like the top bun, PAS is like the bottom bun, and the verb is like the hamburger in the middle.

PARTS OF SPEECH

57

Check your answers using Appendix 2: Answer Key.

TRY THIS!

Decide whether each sentence is positive or negative. Then, change the positive sentences into negative sentences and the negative sentences into positive sentences.

- Il parle beaucoup.
- Vous habitez sur la rue Lafayette.
- Nous ne mangeons pas vite.
- Je nage dans la piscine.
- Tu n'achètes pas le livre.

Asking a Question

When we ask someone a question, we often add a question word at the beginning. The most common way to ask a question is by adding EST-CE QUE at the beginning.

Est-ce que tu vas en vacances ?
(Are you going on a holiday?)
Est-ce que ta sœur fait des biscuits ?
(Is your sister making cookies?)

When EST-CE QUE precedes a vowel, drop the E and add an apostrophe.

Est-ce qu'ils aiment la pizza?
(Do they like pizza?)

Some other common question words are:
- Combien de ? (How many?)
- Comment ? (How?)
- Pourquoi ? (Why?)
- Quand ? (When?)
- Où ? (Where?)
- Que or Qu' ? (What?)
- Quel/Quelle/Quels/Quelles ? (Which?)
- Qui ? (Who?)

When you use all these question words, except for QUI, you also need to use EST-CE QUE.

Combien de pupitres est-ce qu'il y a dans la salle de classe ?
(How many desks are in the classroom?)

Combien de bonbons ?

Comment est-ce que madame D'Ambrosio va au travail ?
(How does Mrs. D'Ambrosio go to work?)

Qui fait du bruit ?
(Who is making noise?)

TRY THIS!

- Write three questions using three different question words.

IT'S A WRAP!

- In these sentences, find the subject and the verb. Identify the other words. They could be:
  - nouns
  - adjectives
  - possessive adjectives
  - adverbs
  - prepositions
  - interjections
  - definite articles
  - indefinite articles
  - conjunctions
  - question words

  > Aïe ! J'ai trop de devoirs.

  > Mon manteau est sous la chaise bleue.

  > Je suis très contente parce que je vais chez ma grand-mère.

  > Quand est-ce que ton père achète une nouvelle auto ?

  > J'ai un beau chandail rouge.

- Make up sentences in French to describe:
  > how you travel to school each day;
  > a garden in the spring; and
  > something that happens in a novel you have read.

  In each sentence, use as many parts of speech as you can.

Check your answers using Appendix 2: Answer Key.

ADULTS CAN HELP

- When your child writes or says a noun, ask him or her what article should be in front of it (le, la, les, un, une, des).
- Provide opportunities for your child to practise using new words in a sentence rather than just listing a series of words or conjugating verbs. For example, ask your child what is done in a kitchen. Encourage him or her to answer in complete sentences.
- The more children use French, the more they'll remember and learn. In school, students are encouraged to speak in French even if they make mistakes. If we stop to correct everything, we can quickly destroy their spontaneity and confidence. Encourage your child to talk to you in French or write you short notes. Praise the effort, even if he or she makes mistakes.

Part 4: How to Communicate in French

Chapter 1: Listening

French is all around you, though you may have to look for it a little depending on where you live. It's on the radio and TV, it's in the bookstore, it's on package labels, it's in school, and it's in the streets. How can you understand all this French? How can you communicate in French?

The first step is to become a good listener. There are many things you can listen to, including CDs, DVDs, your teacher, the radio, and TV. You'll have trouble understanding at first. You won't know a lot of the words and everything's going to sound really fast. Use the strategies on pages 61–62 to build your listening skills; it will get easier.

Strategies Good Listeners Use

Use your ears.

- **Listen for words you know:** Listen to your French teacher, a CD, or a DVD. What words do you recognize from French class? Do you hear words that sound just like they do in English?
- **Don't worry about words you don't know:** Don't stop if you hear a word you don't know. Just listen to the rest of the sentence. It may help you figure out the word you didn't understand.
- **Listen to the tone of voice:** Sometimes you can figure out what a person is saying by listening to his or her tone. Does the person seem angry? Happy? Calm? Excited?
- **Listen for pronunciation:** Listen carefully when you hear words pronounced so that, when you use the same words, you'll pronounce them correctly.

Use your eyes.

- **Watch body language:** A person's body language will often tell you if he or she is happy, angry, sad, frustrated, etc. Gestures are also important; try to figure out what they mean.
- **Look at the visuals:** Pictures, maps, photographs, and other visuals will help you understand what is being said.
- **Visualize:** Sometimes you can hear better when you close your eyes. You won't be distracted by the sights around you and you'll be able to concentrate on listening.
- **Watch the mouth:** The position of a person's lips will help you figure out how to pronounce different sounds.

Use your brain.

- **Identify proper nouns:** Listen for names of people and places. This will give you an idea of who is involved in the action and where the action is taking place.

- **Identify the main idea:** Listen for words that are repeated or emphasized. Look at any visuals that accompany what you are listening to. If you're doing the listening activity in class, think about the questions the teacher asked you before the activity started. These will often be about the main idea.

- **Take notes:** Use a graphic organizer to help you remember the details you heard. See pages 74–76 for examples of graphic organizers. In addition, sometimes in class you'll fill out an activity sheet when you listen. This helps you remember the details, and you can use it like a note page.

Listen again.

- **Listen more than once:** Whenever you can, ask to have a CD played more than once or play a DVD frequently. This will help you get used to the sounds of the language. You'll hear something new each time you listen, and you'll develop your listening skills faster the more you listen.

- **Repeat:** If you can, repeat what you've heard. Your teacher has you repeat a lot in class. This helps you remember the pronunciation and intonation. (See pages 67–68 for more information about intonation.)

Things to Listen To

- If you and your family watch TV or listen to the radio, try watching and listening to Radio-Canada, the CBC's French network, even if it's only for a few minutes each day. Radio-Canada is available across the country.

- Listen to French CDs and watch French DVDs or English DVDs that have a French language option. You can find these in your local library, bookstore, or music store. Choose a variety — some stories, some cartoons, some songs. Be patient when you listen to them. At first you won't understand everything, but the more you listen the more you'll understand. And, if you're watching a DVD, you'll still know what it's about because you can follow along with the pictures.

- Don't forget that your best source for French in school is your teacher. Listen carefully when the teacher speaks French and try to imitate her or him. French is a very musical language, so listen to hear the sounds and the intonation, or the way your teacher's voice goes up and down when speaking. (See pages 67–68 for more information about intonation.) Don't be afraid to ask for help or to ask your teacher to repeat a word.

TRY THIS!

Find someone speaking French on TV, on the radio, on the Internet, on a podcast, or on a DVD. Listen for a couple of minutes. What words or phrases do you recognize? What do you notice about the way the language sounds?

Chapter 2 Reading

You'll find French to read all around you: labels, packaging, pamphlets, brochures, posters, magazines, catalogues, and so on. You'll find some of these in class, but look outside of school too. At first you may not understand a lot of what you read, unless it's in your French class. Like listening, there are strategies to help you learn to read French.

Strategies Good Readers Use

Use what you already know.

- **Look for words you already know:** Most of the time, what you read will have words that you learned in class. Find those words; they'll help you understand the rest of the text.

- **Look for cognates:** Cognates are words that are identical or similar to English words; for example, December and *décembre*; telephone and *téléphone*.

- **Look for words from the same family:** Words that have the same root word are considered words from the same family. For example, you know the verb *finir*, to finish. If you see the words *la fin, final, finalement,* and *fini,* you might be able to figure out what they mean because they have the same root and are from the same family as *finir*.

"Soupe" and "soup" are cognates. So are "tomates" and "tomatoes."

"Restaurant" is spelled the same in French and English.

Use the whole page.

- **Look at the visuals:** There are often pictures and illustrations that show what the story or reading passage is all about. Use the visuals to help you understand.

- **Read the title and subtitles:** This will help you predict what the reading selection will be about.

- **Look at the context:** Think about the words you see. If you think you know what they mean, try to figure out if they make sense in the context of what you're reading. If not, think about what else they might mean.

- **Look for the main idea:** Find the main idea and supporting details. The title, subtitles, and illustrations will help you.

Think ahead.

- **Make predictions:** Try to predict what the story is going to be about and what will happen next. Use the visuals to help you.

Try other strategies.

- **Reread:** If you don't understand something the first time you read it, read it again. Sometimes something at the end of the story can help you figure out the beginning.
- **Visualize:** Closing your eyes can help you "see" the details of the reading selection in your mind and help you better understand what you're reading.

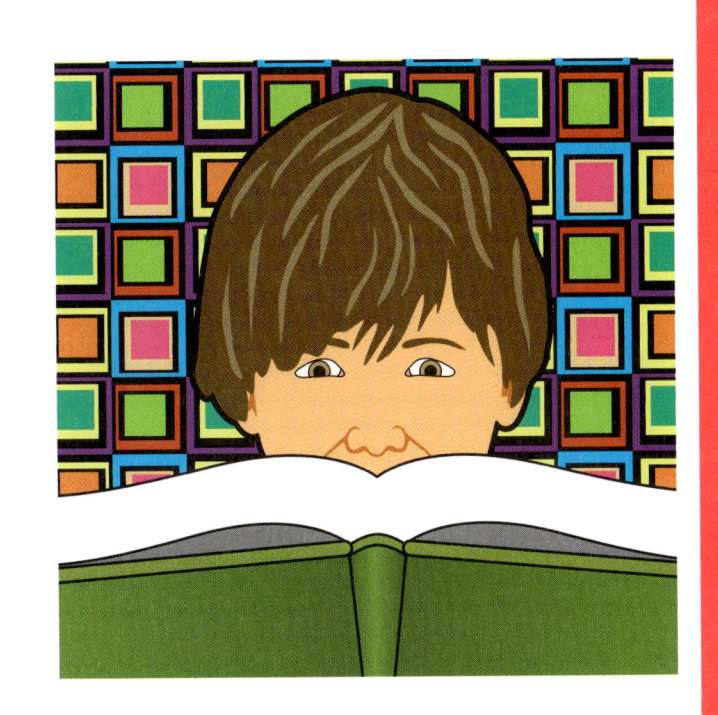

Things to Read

- Everywhere you go, check pamphlets, brochures, magazines, signs, etc. You'll be amazed at how much French is around you. Remember that Canadian stores, banks, and government offices often have French pamphlets. If you're in a chain store with your parents, ask someone who works there if they have French pamphlets, catalogues, etc. If they don't, they may be able to order some for you from their head office or from one of their Quebec stores.
- Check out the websites of Éditions Scholastic, Radio-Canada, French newspapers such as *La Presse* and *Le Devoir*, government departments, and French businesses. These websites have lots for you to read, as well as games to play and activities to try. You'll be amazed at how much of the French you understand. Use the strategies you've learned to figure out words and ideas that you don't know.
- Check out some of the resources listed in Appendix 1: Useful Resources, on pages 96–97.

TRY THIS!

Look for French on a brochure, newspaper, or website printout. Circle the words you already know. Underline the words you can figure out using the strategies you learned. Summarize what you read in one or two English sentences or try summarizing it using your own words in French.

Chapter 3: Speaking

Learning to speak a new language can be a lot of fun. Speak in class, practise at home, and teach your family, friends, and neighbours if you can. To be a good French speaker, you also have to be a good listener and reader. You'll learn new words, hear how to pronounce them, and figure out what they mean in a context.

Strategies Good Speakers Use

Learn by listening.

- **Pay attention to the intonation:** French is a musical language. Your voice goes up and down as you speak. So listen carefully when someone speaks to you and imitate the sounds you hear. See pages 67–68 for more information about intonation.

- **Learn the words you need:** The more French words you have at your fingertips, the more you'll be able to talk to someone. Every day in class, you'll learn new words. Try to remember them. Pay attention to the French words you see out of class too.

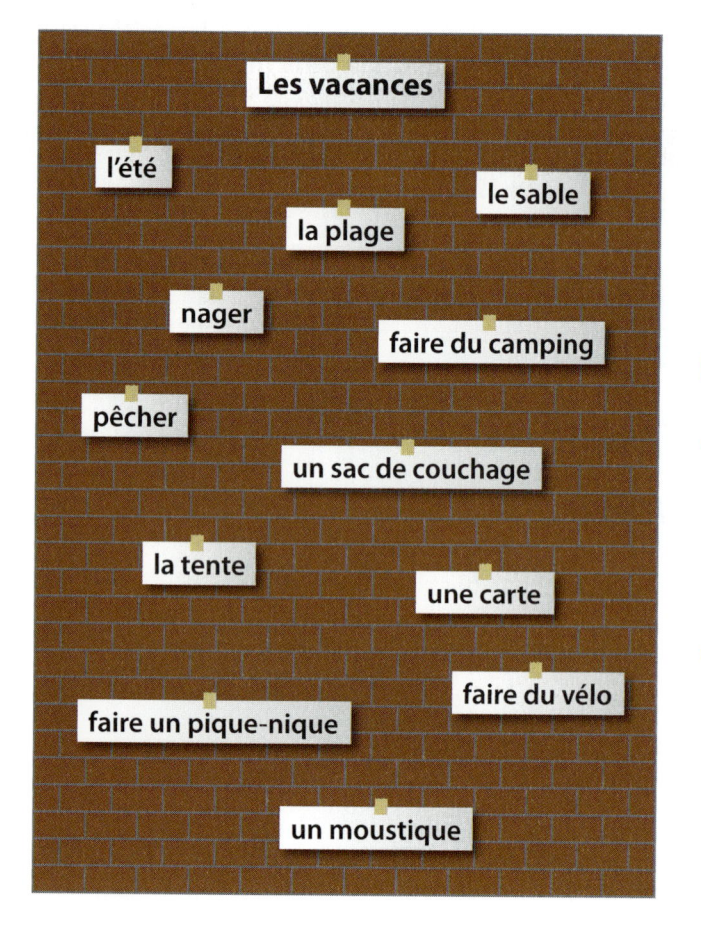

Learn by reading.

- **Learn new words:** Check the class word wall and the notes the teacher leaves on the board. Check the words you've written in your workbook and do your best to remember as many as you can. The more you use them, the more you'll remember them.

Learn by speaking.

- **Practise in front of a mirror:** Watch your lips form the different sounds. You may feel like you're exaggerating, but that's because French sounds very different from English. If you make your French words sound like English, you're probably not pronouncing them correctly.

- **Practise pronouncing cognates:** Cognates are French words that are similar to English words. Practise saying "telephone" in English and *téléphone* in French. Try "rhinoceros" and *rhinocéros*. The words in each pair look similar, but there are small differences in their spellings that change the way they're pronounced. The different way that R is said in French changes the pronunciation too.

Les vacances
l'été
le sable
la plage
nager
faire du camping
pêcher
un sac de couchage
la tente
une carte
faire un pique-nique
faire du vélo
un moustique

- **Check Part 2: The Letter:** Reread Part 2: The Letter and the Pronunciation Guide on pages 81–83 to remind yourself how to pronounce individual letters and combinations of letters.
- **Practise:** You'll have many opportunities to speak French in class, but if you have other chances to speak French during the day, don't be afraid to do so.
- **Repeat:** Your French teacher will ask you to repeat often; this helps you pronounce the words properly.

Intonation

When a French word has more than one syllable, the main stress is always on the last syllable. This is different from English.

ENGLISH	FRENCH
sand′ wich	sand wich′
tel′ e phone	té lé phone′
tel′ e vi sion	té lé vi sion′
tem′ per a ture	tem pé ra ture′

With sentences, the intonation depends a great deal on the punctuation. Read the sentences below in the way the diagrams suggest.

- The voice goes up in the middle of a sentence. It also goes up when there's a comma. The voice goes down at the end of a sentence with a period.

    Le petit chien, le gros chat, et le garçon sont dans la cour d'école.

- The voice goes up at the end of a sentence that ends with a question mark.

    Qu'est-ce que tu fais dans la cour d'école, Marc ?

- The voice goes down with emphasis when the sentence ends with an exclamation point.

    Je joue avec mon chien, maman !

HOW TO COMMUNICATE IN FRENCH

Check your answers using Appendix 2: Answer Key.

TRY THIS!

Try saying these sentences using the correct intonation.

- Marcel et son ami Jean-Louis vont au cinéma samedi après-midi.
- Monsieur Duval est notre prof aujourd'hui. Pourquoi ? Est-ce que madame Thériault est malade ?
- C'est dimanche et nous allons chez grand-mère pour souper.
- Ma sœur a un nouveau chandail bleu. Il est très beau.
- Sarah a un nouveau poisson. De quelle couleur est son poisson ?
- Le chien chasse la balle. Il court très vite !
- Au souper, je mange une salade, des spaghettis, du pain et au dessert, de la crème glacée. Ouf ! J'ai trop mangé !

TRY THIS!

- Here are some simple conversations to try with a friend or family member. Add a sentence to each one.

Reread the conversations. This time, replace the underlined words with words that apply to you.

- Bonne fête, <u>Natasha.</u>
- Merci, <u>Sandra.</u>
- Quel âge as-tu ?
- Aujourd'hui j'ai <u>10</u> ans.
- Moi, j'ai <u>9</u> ans, mais <u>mon frère</u> a <u>14</u> ans.

Qu'est-ce que tu aimes manger pour le souper ?

J'aime la pizza. Et toi ?

Moi aussi, j'aime la pizza. Mais j'aime aussi les spaghettis.

Qu'est-ce que tu prends comme dessert ?

J'aime les fruits, mais j'aime aussi la crème glacée.

J'aime les spaghettis.

J'aime la pizza.

- Interview a friend, close neighbour, or family member. Ask about his/her name, age, likes, and dislikes. Then tell another friend, close neighbour, or family member about the person you interviewed. Follow this model:

  Je vous présente _____.

  Il/elle s'appelle _____.

  Il/elle habite _____.

  Il/elle aime _____.

  Il/elle n'aime pas _____.

  Son sport préféré est _____.

  Son passe-temps préféré est _____.

- Using the words and expressions you know, create a short conversation with a friend or family member about one of these themes.
  - ton animal de compagnie
  - les sports
  - l'école
  - la maison
  - les saisons et les vêtements

  Look in Commonly Used Words on pages 84–95 for words that you may be able to use in your conversation.

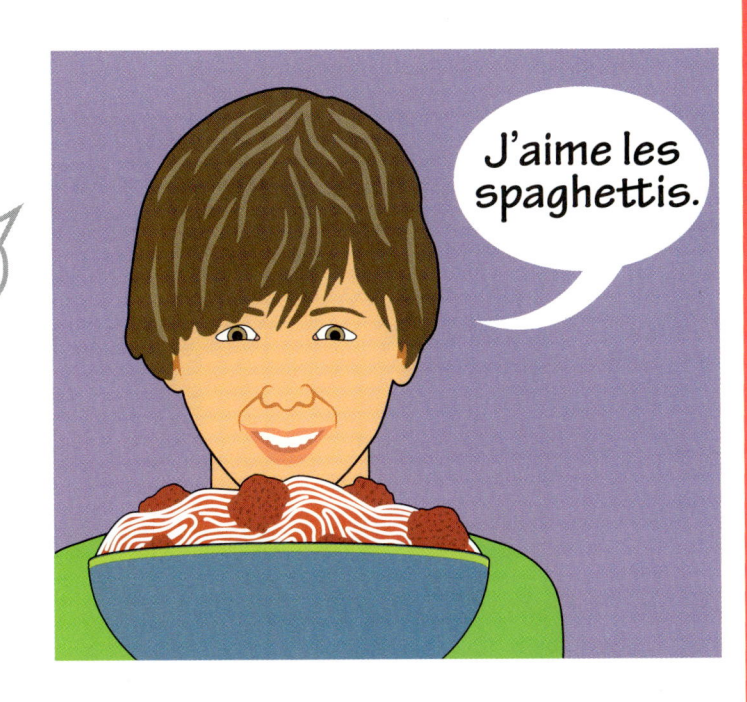

HOW TO COMMUNICATE IN FRENCH

Some Common Expressions for Conversations

Bonjour ! Salut !	Hello! Hi!
Au revoir !	Bye!
À demain.	See you tomorrow.
Bonne journée !	Enjoy your day! Have a good day!
Quel âge as-tu ? (J'ai . . . ans.)	How old are you? (I'm . . . years old.)
Quelle heure est-il ? (Il est . . .)	What time is it? (It's . . .)
Comment t'appelles-tu ?	What's your name?
(Je m'appelle . . .)	(My name is . . .)
Comment ça va ?	How are you?
(Ça va très bien.)	(I'm very well.)
(Pas mal.)	(Not bad.)
Merci.	Thank you.
De rien.	You're welcome.
S'il vous plaît.	Please.
Excuse-moi.	Excuse me.

- Play word games with your family and friends to help you build your French vocabulary. You can use a French-English dictionary if you wish.

  ▶ Say a word, then challenge everyone else to say a word that rhymes with it. Here are some examples of rhyming words:

mère	**père**	**frère**
chien	**bien**	**rien**
je	**ne**	**de**
gâteau	**bateau**	**château**
main	**train**	**pain**

  ▶ Say a word, then ask the next person to say a word that begins with the last letter of the word you said. For example:

  maison → **numéro** → **oeuf** → **famille** →
  et → **table** → **enfant** → **tête**

▶ Play the Suitcase Game. Begin by saying this sentence starter: "Je vais en vacances et dans ma valise je mets . . ." ("I'm going on holiday and in my suitcase I'm putting . . ."). Finish the sentence by naming one item you're going to put in your suitcase. Don't forget to include LE, LA, LES, UN, UNE, or DES when you're naming the item.

When you're done your turn, ask the next person to repeat the sentence starter, tell what you took, then add one item. Keep playing until you lose track of what's in the suitcase.

Here's an example of a very long sentence:

Je vais en vacances et dans ma valise je mets des souliers, un manteau, un pantalon, une chemise, un livre, un biscuit, une télévision, une banane, une fleur, une photo . . .

HOW TO COMMUNICATE IN FRENCH

Chapter 4

Writing

When you first learn to write in French, your teacher will give you words and sentences to copy and complete. This will help you develop the knowledge and vocabulary you need to write on your own. Once you know several words and expressions, your teacher will ask you to listen and write down what you hear. This will help you remember what words look like and how to write them.

Just like good English writing, good French writing has correct word choices and spellings, proper sentences, creative ideas, and strong organization. As you begin to write, you will focus on using correct words and spellings and building sentences. When you're more confident, use what you learn about organizing ideas in English writing to help you write in French.

Strategies Good Writers Use

Spell accurately.

- **Copy words carefully:** Changing the spelling might change the meaning of a word. Don't forget to check for accents.

- **Look it up:** If you want to add a word that you know to your writing but can't remember how to spell it, look it up in Commonly Used Words on pages 84–95, in your French textbook, or in a dictionary.

- **Remember the articles:** Remember that all nouns are preceded by words like LE, LA, LES, UN, UNE, and DES. Don't forget to put them in.

Choose the right words.

- **Look at the context:** When you have to choose a word from a list to complete a sentence and you're not sure which one to choose, eliminate the words that don't fit the context. You'll be left with a shorter list to choose from.

- **Look it up:** Your teacher will rarely ask you to write words you've never seen or learned. If you can't remember a word, check the glossary at the back of your book, look for the word in Commonly Used Words on pages 84–95, reread work you've done in class, or use a French-English dictionary to find the word.

- **Visual dictionaries:** Visual dictionaries are an excellent way to remember new vocabulary. If you can't buy one, create your own. Divide a sheet of paper into six boxes and draw a picture or paste a photograph of something you want to remember in each box. Write the French word under the illustration or photo. Don't forget to put LE or LA in front of the word to remind you if it's masculine or feminine. Keep a scrapbook of your visuals and, before long, you'll have your own visual dictionary. **Hint:** Divide your illustrations according to themes: *les sports, les articles dans la cuisine, les activités après l'école, les membres de la famille, les animaux*, etc. This will make it easier for you find the illustrations and words you need.

Build sentences.

- **Follow the model carefully:** As you begin to write in French, you'll usually follow a model. Build your sentences using the patterns you see in the model. If you'd like to add originality to your writing, use sentence structures and words you've already learned.

- **Use your reading as a model:** When you read, look carefully at how the words work together. Keep an eye out for new words and take note of how they're spelled. Try to remember them in case you need them for a writing assignment.

Abbreviations

Abbreviations are shortened forms of words. They are made by leaving out letters or replacing a group of letters with another letter or symbol.

Here are some common abbreviations that you might use when you write:

Mme	**Madame** (Mrs.)		**M.**	**Monsieur** (Mr.)
Mlle	**Mademoiselle** (Miss)		**prof.**	**professeur** (professor)
Dr	**Docteur** (Dr.)			

HOW TO COMMUNICATE IN FRENCH

Take notes.

- **Use graphic organizers, just like you do in your English class.** Try webs, Venn diagrams, fishbones, Know—Want to Know—Learned (Savoir—Veux Savoir—Appris) charts, and T-charts. Ask your teacher for these if you don't have any blank ones, or create your own.

  ▶ A **web** helps you focus on the main vocabulary and other words that go with it.

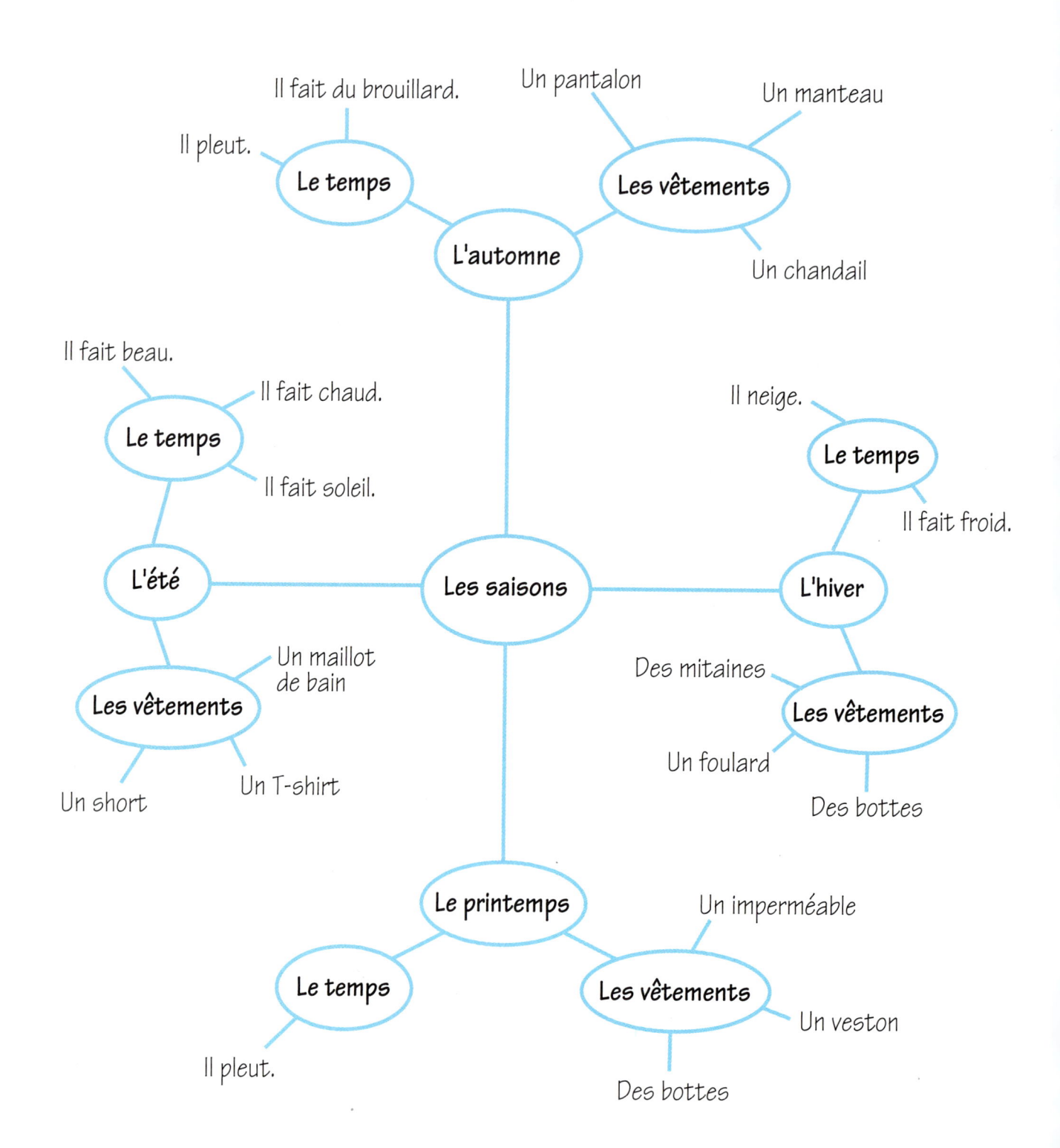

L'automne
- Le temps
  - Il pleut.
  - Il fait du brouillard.
- Les vêtements
  - Un pantalon
  - Un manteau
  - Un chandail

L'été
- Le temps
  - Il fait beau.
  - Il fait chaud.
  - Il fait soleil.
- Les vêtements
  - Un maillot de bain
  - Un T-shirt
  - Un short

L'hiver
- Le temps
  - Il neige.
  - Il fait froid.
- Les vêtements
  - Des mitaines
  - Un foulard
  - Des bottes

Le printemps
- Le temps
  - Il pleut.
- Les vêtements
  - Un imperméable
  - Un veston
  - Des bottes

Central node: **Les saisons**

▶ A **Venn diagram** helps you identify similarities and differences.

La vie dans la ville | La vie à la campagne

- de grands magasins
- beaucoup de gens
- beaucoup de voitures
- de grandes écoles

- un chien
- un chat
- des jardins
- des maisons

- des chevaux
- des vaches
- des fermes
- de petites écoles

▶ A **fishbone** helps you identify main ideas and supporting details.

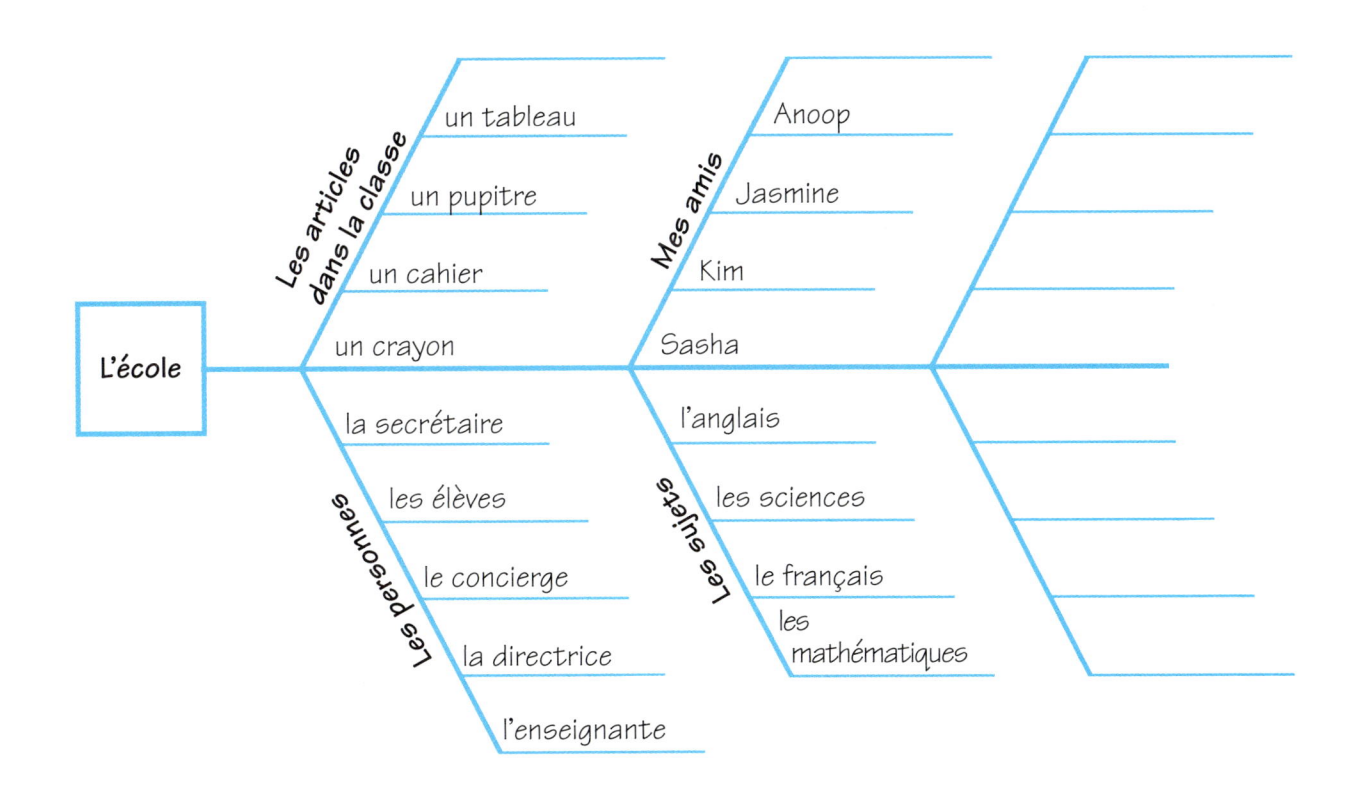

L'école

Les articles dans la classe:
- un tableau
- un pupitre
- un cahier
- un crayon

Mes amis:
- Anoop
- Jasmine
- Kim
- Sasha

Les personnes:
- la secrétaire
- les élèves
- le concierge
- la directrice
- l'enseignante

Les sujets:
- l'anglais
- les sciences
- le français
- les mathématiques

HOW TO COMMUNICATE IN FRENCH

75

▶ A **KWL** (SVA) chart shows things you **k**now (**S**avoir), things you **w**ant to know (**V**eux savoir), and things you **l**earned after doing research (**A**ppris).

CARNAVAL

Savoir	Veux Savoir	Appris
Bonhomme est le symbole du Carnaval.	Qu'est-ce que Bonhomme porte ?	Il porte une ceinture fléchée.

▶ A **T-chart** helps you organize your thoughts about two sides of an issue.

ACHETER UN CHIEN

Pour	Contre
Un chien est un ami.	Je dois souvent promener le chien.
Je peux jouer avec un chien.	Les chiens mangent des choses autour de la maison.

TRY THIS!

- Create a web called *Les animaux*. Use words you know to show categories of animals, names of animals, and other things you know about them.
- Make a French card for a friend or family member. Here are examples of cards you might make. Also, see page 85 for the names of holidays for which you might want to make cards.

BONNE FÊTE

JOYEUX NOËL

BONNE FÊTE DES PÈRES

MERCI

HOW TO COMMUNICATE IN FRENCH

77

- Use these models to help you write an identity (ID) card, an e-mail, and a postcard.

▶ An ID Card (Une carte d'identité)

A student from another school prepared this ID card. Follow the model to create your own ID card. If you'd like, you can just replace the underlined words with words that work for you.

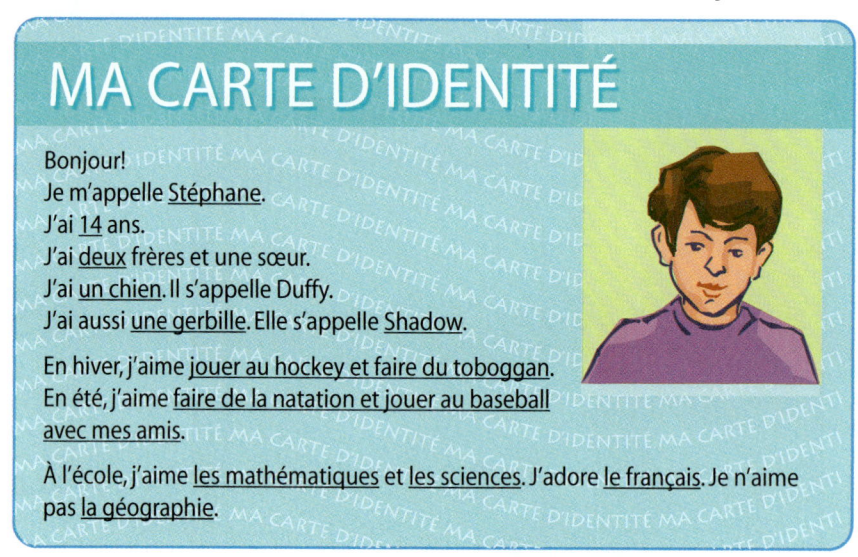

MA CARTE D'IDENTITÉ

Bonjour!
Je m'appelle <u>Stéphane</u>.
J'ai <u>14</u> ans.
J'ai <u>deux</u> frères et une sœur.
J'ai <u>un chien</u>. Il s'appelle Duffy.
J'ai aussi <u>une gerbille</u>. Elle s'appelle <u>Shadow</u>.

En hiver, j'aime <u>jouer au hockey et faire du toboggan</u>.
En été, j'aime <u>faire de la natation et jouer au baseball avec mes amis</u>.

À l'école, j'aime <u>les mathématiques</u> et <u>les sciences</u>. J'adore <u>le français</u>. Je n'aime pas <u>la géographie</u>.

▶ An E-mail (Un courriel)

Nadia sent this e-mail to her grandmother. Use the guidelines in blue to help you write an e-mail to someone you know.

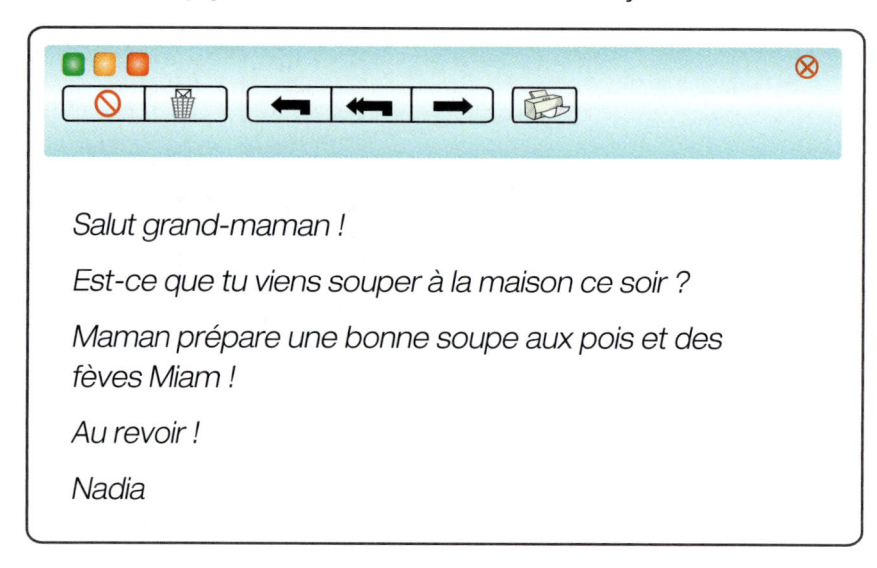

À qui est-ce que tu écris ton courriel ?

Quel est ton message ?

Qu'est-ce que tu demandes à la personne ?

Dis merci ou au revoir.

Écris ton nom.

Salut grand-maman !

Est-ce que tu viens souper à la maison ce soir ?

Maman prépare une bonne soupe aux pois et des fèves Miam !

Au revoir !

Nadia

▶ **A Postcard (Une carte postale)**

Use the guidelines in blue to help you write a postcard to someone you know. Use Jean-François' postcard as a model. You can imagine you are writing from anywhere you'd like.

Dis bonjour.

Où es-tu ?
Qu'est-ce que tu fais ?

Dis au revoir.

Écris ton nom.

Bonjour maman ! Bonjour papa !

Je suis à Shediac avec Paul-Émile et sa famille.
Je joue au football et au baseball. Je nage dans l'océan.
Je mange du homard. Miam ! C'est bon avec du beurre.

Au revoir !
Je vous embrasse !

Jean-François

Luc Robitaille et Solange Pépin
26, rue Seaborne
St-Gustave (Québec)
H1J 1K4

À qui est-ce que tu écris ta carte postale ?

IT'S A WRAP!

Listening, reading, writing, and speaking work together. You can't speak or write until you've learned some words by listening and reading. Here's a reminder of some things you can do to help you communicate in French.

- Practise speaking in front of a mirror.
- Listen carefully when you hear words pronounced. Imitate the sounds as closely as possible.
- Listen to a CD or watch a DVD more than once. You'll learn new words each time.
- When you write according to a model, follow the model very closely.
- Look at your visual dictionary and at the classroom word wall to help you when you speak and write.
- Take good notes when you listen and read. Keep them in a binder that you can use as a reference all year long.

HOW TO COMMUNICATE IN FRENCH

ADULTS CAN HELP

- Encourage your child to watch 5–10 minutes of French TV a few times a week. You might also record some young people's after-school programs so that your child can watch the same program more than once. Watching and listening help students attune their ears to the sounds of French and learn new words.
- Check out the Internet for French podcasts your child can listen to.
- Play card games, like Concentration, in French. Your child will appreciate teaching you the French vocabulary you need to play.
- Many computer games for young people are available in French. Ask your child's French teacher for recommendations.
- If possible, purchase books that are accompanied by CDs so that your child can listen to the story while following along in the book. This will help your child learn new vocabulary and attune his or her ear to the sounds of French.
- There are many French comic books and cartoons that your child will enjoy. If possible, watch a DVD or read a book about Tintin, Astérix, or Lucky Luke, all cartoon characters made famous in Europe.
- Allow your child to post little sticky notes with French words for household items around the house. Remind him or her to identify if the word is masculine or feminine. Test your child and let him or her test you.
- Help your child create a visual dictionary.

Part 5: Building Your Vocabulary

Chapter 1: Pronunciation Guide

The charts on pages 81–83 show you how to pronounce different French sounds.

SPELLING	APPROXIMATE ENGLISH PRONUNCIATION	SAMPLE FRENCH WORDS
a, â	"a" in c**a**t	**a**ttention, **â**ge
ai, aî	"e" in l**e**t	fr**ai**s, fr**aî**che
ai	"ay" in "w**ay**"	**ai**mer
ain	"e" in **e**nter (nasal)	dem**ain**
an	"a" in w**a**nt (nasal)	d**an**se
au	"o" in n**o**se	ch**au**d
b	"b" in **b**oy	**b**alance
c	"c" in **c**amel	é**c**outer
c, ç	"s" in **S**unday	**c**iseaux, fran**ç**ais
ch	"sh" in **sh**oe	**ch**eval
d	"d" in **d**aily	**d**anser
e, è, ê, ei	"e" in l**e**t	l**e**ttre, apr**è**s, t**ê**te, tr**ei**ze
e, eu, eux	"oo" in b**oo**k	l**e**, h**eu**r**eux**
é, er, ez	"ay" in w**ay**	fâch**é**, parl**er**, n**ez**

SPELLING	APPROXIMATE ENGLISH PRONUNCIATION	SAMPLE FRENCH WORDS
eau	"o" in n**o**se	mant**eau**
ein	"e" in **e**nter (nasal)	pl**ein**
en, em	"o" in **o**n (nasal)	cont**en**t, t**em**ps
et	"e" in l**e**t	**et**
f	"f" in **f**all	che**f**
g	"g" in **g**row	**g**rand
ge	"g" in colla**ge**	rou**ge**
gn	"ny" ca**ny**on (nasal)	oi**gn**on
h	always silent in French	**h**ockey
i, î, ï, ie	"ee" in str**ee**t	r**i**che, **î**le, ma**ï**s, v**ie**
in	"e" in **e**nter (nasal)	mat**in**
j	"g" in colla**ge**	**j**aune
k	"k" in ban**k**	**k**ilomètre
l	"l" in **l**ove	**l**ivre
ll	"ll" in "caller"	a**ll**ons
ll	"y" in **y**ou	fami**ll**e
m	"m" in **m**om	**m**a**m**an
n	"n" in **n**ever	**n**euf
o, ô	"o" in d**o**nut	m**o**t, h**ô**pital
o	"o" in h**o**rrible	h**o**rizon
oi	"wha" in **wha**t	**oi**seau
om, on	"o" in ph**o**ne (nasal)	p**om**pier, l**on**g
ou	"oo" in r**oo**m	**ou**vrir
p	"p" in **p**otato	**p**apa
ph	"ph" in telep**h**one	télé**ph**one
qu	"k" in **k**ing	**qu**el
r	"r" in **r**aven (rolling sound)	**r**at

82

SPELLING	APPROXIMATE ENGLISH PRONUNCIATION	SAMPLE FRENCH WORDS
s	"z" in **z**ebra	tré**s**or
s, sc, ss, ti	"s" in **s**erious	**s**ouper, **sc**iences, poi**ss**on, opéra**ti**on
t, th	"t" in **t**omato	**t**able, **th**é
u, û, ue	"ew" in gr**ew**	**u**niforme, fl**û**te, r**ue**
ue	"oo" in b**oo**k	q**ue**
ui	"wee" in **wee**d	c**ui**sine
un, um	"eu" in s**u**n (nasal)	**un**, parf**um**
v, w	"v" in **v**ery	**v**acances, **w**agon
w	"w" in **w**ater	**w**eekend
x	"x" in e**x**amine	e**x**emple
x	"cks" in so**cks**	e**x**cité
y	"y" in **y**ou	**y**oga
y	"ee" in str**ee**t	c**y**cle
z	"z" in **z**ebra	**z**éro

BUILDING YOUR VOCABULARY

Chapter 2 Commonly Used Words

This chapter is like your own dictionary, with words you can use every day.

Days, Months, Seasons

DAYS OF THE WEEK

lundi	Monday	vendredi	Friday
mardi	Tuesday	samedi	Saturday
mercredi	Wednesday	dimanche	Sunday
jeudi	Thursday		

TIMES OF THE DAY

le matin	morning	Il est huit heures.	It's 8:00.
l'après-midi (*m.*)	afternoon	Il est huit heures et quart.	It's 8:15.
le soir	evening	Il est huit heures trente./ Il est huit heures et demi.	It's 8:30.
la nuit	night	Il est neuf heures moins le quart./ Il est huit heures quarante-cinq.	It's a quarter to nine./ It's 8:45.

MONTHS OF THE YEAR

janvier	January	juillet	July
février	Febuary	août	August
mars	March	septembre	September
avril	April	octobre	October
mai	May	novembre	November
juin	June	décembre	December

SEASONS

| le printemps | spring | l'automne (*m.*) | autumn, fall |
| l'été (*m.*) | summer | l'hiver (*m.*) | winter |

The Weather

Il fait soleil.	It's sunny.	Il pleut.	It's raining.
Il fait nuageux.	It's cloudy.	Il fait humide.	It's humid.
Il fait beau.	It's nice.	Il neige.	It's snowing.
Il fait mauvais.	It's bad out.	Il fait du brouillard.	It's foggy.
Il fait chaud.	It's hot.	Il fait du vent./Il vente.	It's windy.
Il fait froid.	It's cold.	Il fait –10°C.	It's –10°C.

Holidays

la fête	holiday	la fête des Pères	Father's Day
les vacances	vacation	les vacances d'été	summer vacation
le jour de l'An	New Year's Day	l'Halloween (*m.*)	Halloween
le Carnaval	Carnival	le jour du Souvenir	Remembrance Day
la Saint-Valentin	Valentine's Day	la Sainte-Catherine	Saint Catherine's Day
la Saint-Patrick	Saint Patrick's Day	le Noël	Christmas
les vacances de printemps	spring break	le Ramadan	Ramadan
la fête des Mères	Mother's Day	la Hanoukka	Hanukah

School Words

SCHOOL SUBJECTS

l'anglais (*m.*)	English	les mathématiques	math
les arts (*m., pl.*)	art	la musique	music
l'éducation physique (*f.*)	gym	la récréation	recess
le français	French	la religion	religion
la géographie	geography	les sciences (*f., pl.*)	science
l'histoire (*f.*)	history		

BUILDING YOUR VOCABULARY

THINGS AT SCHOOL

l'affiche (f.)	poster	le gymnase	gym
l'aide enseignant	male teacher's aide	le haut-parleur	speaker (for announcements)
l'aide enseignante	female teacher's aide	l'horloge (f.)	clock
l'autobus (m.)	bus	le lecteur de disques	CD player
le bureau	teacher's desk, office	le lecteur de DVD	DVD player
la cafétéria	cafeteria, lunch room	le livre	book
le cahier	workbook	le magnétoscope	VCR
le calendrier	calendar	le marqueur	marker
la carte éclair	flashcard	l'ordinateur (m.)	computer
le clavier	keyboard	le papier	paper
le crayon	pencil	le plafond	ceiling
le crayon de couleur	coloured pencil	le plancher	floor
les devoirs (m., pl.)	homework	la plante	plant
le directeur	male principal	la porte	door
la directrice	female principal	le professeur/le prof	male teacher
le directeur adjoint	male vice principal	la professeure/la prof	female teacher
la directrice adjointe	female vice principal	le projecteur	projector
le disque compact	CD	le pupitre	desk
le DVD	DVD	la récréation	recess
l'écran (m.)	computer screen	le stylo	pen
l'élève (m. & f.)	student	le tableau	blackboard
l'enseignant	male teacher	le tableau d'affichage	bulletin board
l'enseignante	female teacher	la télévision	TV
la fenêtre	window	le terrain	schoolyard
le film	film		

Sports

le badminton	badminton	le patinage	skating
le baseball	baseball	le ski alpin	downhill skiing
le basket-ball	basketball	le ski de fond	cross country skiing
le canotage	canoeing	le ski nautique	water skiing
le cyclisme	cycling	le snowboard	snowboarding
le football	football	le soccer	soccer
le hockey	hockey	le tennis	tennis
la natation	swimming	le volley-ball	volleyball

About Me

PARTS OF MY BODY

la bouche	mouth	la main	hand
le bras	arm	le menton	chin
le corps	body	le nez	nose
le cou	neck	l'œil (*m.*), les yeux (*m., pl.*)	eye, eyes
le coude	elbow	l'oreille (*f.*)	ear
le doigt	finger	l'orteil (*m.*)	toe
le dos	back	le pied	foot
l'épaule (*f.*)	shoulder	la poitrine	chest
l'estomac (*m.*)	stomach	le pouce	thumb
la jambe	leg	la tête	head
la langue	tongue	le ventre	belly
la lèvre	lip	le visage/la figure	face

HOW I'M FEELING

Comment ça va ?	How are you?/How's it going?	J'ai mal à la tête.	I have a headache.
Ça va bien.	I'm doing fine./It's going well.	J'ai chaud.	I'm hot.
Je suis heureux/heureuse.	I'm happy.	J'ai froid.	I'm cold.
Je suis triste.	I'm sad.	J'ai soif.	I'm thirsty.
Je suis fâché/fâchée.	I'm angry.	J'ai faim.	I'm hungry.
Je suis en bonne santé.	I'm healthy.	J'ai peur.	I'm scared.
Je suis fatigué/fatiguée.	I'm tired.		

BUILDING YOUR VOCABULARY

My Neighbourhood

PLACES

l'appartement (*m.*)	apartment	le magasin	store
la banque	bank	la maison	house
la bibliothèque	library	le marché	market
la boulangerie	bakery	la pâtisserie	pastry shop
le café	café	la pharmacie	pharmacy
la caserne des pompiers	fire station	la poste	post office
le centre commercial	shopping centre	le restaurant	restaurant
l'école (*f.*)	school	la rue	street
l'épicerie (*f.*)	butcher	la station de métro	subway stop
la librairie	bookstore	le trottoir	sidewalk

PEOPLE AND PROFESSIONS

l'agent/l'agente de police (*m.; f.*)	police officer	le mécanicien/la mécanicienne	mechanic
l'avocat/l'avocate (*m.; f.*)	lawyer	le docteur/la docteure	doctor
le chauffeur/la chauffeuse d'autobus	bus driver	le/la pilote	pilot
le chauffeur/la chauffeuse de camion	truck driver	le plombier/la plombière	plumber
le coiffeur/la coiffeuse	hairdressser	le pompier/la pompière	firefighter
le/la comptable	accountant	le/la secrétaire	secretary
le facteur/la factrice	letter carrier	le serveur/la serveuse	server
le fermier/la fermière	farmer	le vendeur/la vendeuse	salesperson
l'infirmier/l'infirmière (*m.; f.*)	nurse	le/la vétérinaire	veterinarian

TRANSPORTATION

l'autobus (*m.*)	bus	le métro	subway
l'avion (*m.*)	airplane	la motocyclette	motorcycle
le bateau	boat	le taxi	taxi
la bicyclette	bicycle	le train	train
le camion	truck	la voiture	car
la camionnette	van		

Home Words

THINGS AT HOME

la buanderie	laundry room	la garde-robe	closet
le bureau	office, desk	la lampe	lamp
la chaise	chair	le lit	bed
la chambre à coucher	bedroom	la maison	house
le chat	cat	les rideaux (*m., pl.*)	drapes, curtains
le chien	dog	la salle de bain	bathroom
la cuisine	kitchen	la salle de récréation	recreation room
l'entrée (*f.*)	entrance	le salon	living room
le fauteuil	big, comfortable chair	le sofa	sofa
le foyer	fireplace	le sous-sol	basement
le garage	garage	la table	table

FAMILY MEMBERS

la famille	family	la petite-fille	granddaughter
la mère	mother	la tante	aunt
le père	father	l'oncle	uncle
la fille	daughter	la nièce	niece
le fils	son	le neuveu	nephew
la sœur	sister	la cousine	female cousin
le frère	brother	le cousin	male cousin
le mari	husband	la belle-mère	mother-in-law, stepmother
la femme	wife	le beau-pere	father-in-law, stepfather
la grand-mère	grandmother	la demi-sœur	half sister, stepsister
le grand-père	grandfather	le demi-frère	half brother, stepbrother
le petit-fils	grandson		

Clothing

la blouse	blouse	le manteau	coat
la botte	boot	la mitaine	mitten
le chandail	sweater	le pantalon	pants
le chapeau	hat	la robe	dress
la chaussette	sock	la sandale	sandal
la chemise	shirt	le short	shorts
l'écharpe (*f.*)	scarf	le soulier	shoe
le gant	glove	la tuque	tuque
l'imperméable (*m.*)	raincoat	le T-shirt	t-shirt
la jupe	skirt	le veston	jacket

Food

FRUIT

l'abricot (*m.*)	apricot	le melon	melon
l'ananas (*m.*)	pineapple	la mangue	mango
la baie	berry	l'orange (*f.*)	orange
la banane	banana	le pamplemousse	grapefruit
la cerise	cherry	la pêche	peach
le citron	lemon	la poire	pear
la citrouille	pumpkin	la pomme	apple
la datte	date	la prune	plum
la fraise	strawberry	le raisin	grape
la framboise	raspberry	la tomate	tomato

MEALS

le petit déjeuner	breakfast	le dîner, le souper	dinner
le déjeuner	lunch	la collation	snack

VEGETABLES

l'artichaut (*m.*)	artichoke	la fève	bean
les asperges (*f., pl.*)	asparagus	la laitue	lettuce
l'aubergine (*f.*)	eggplant	le maïs	corn
le brocoli	broccoli	la pomme de terre	potato
la carotte	carrot	l'oignon (*m.*)	onion
le céleri	celery	le petit pois	pea
le champignon	mushroom	le poivron rouge	red pepper
le chou-fleur	cauliflower	le poivron vert	green pepper
le concombre	cucumber	le radis	radish
les épinards (*m., pl.*)	spinach	la salade	salad, lettuce

MEAT, DAIRY, AND MORE

le bacon	bacon	le granola	granola
le biscuit	cookie	le jambon	ham
le bœuf	beef	le lait	milk
le bonbon	candy	la noix	nut
le beurre	butter	l'œuf (*m.*)	egg
le beurre d'arachide	peanut butter	le pain	bread
la céréale	cereal	les pâtes (*f., pl.*)	pasta
le craquelin	cracker	le poisson	fish
la crème	cream	le porc	pork
la crème glacée	ice cream	le poulet	chicken
la crêpe	crêpe	le riz	rice
le fromage	cheese	le toast	toast
le gâteau	cake	le yogourt	yogurt

BUILDING YOUR VOCABULARY

Numbers

zéro	zero	seize	sixteen
un	one	dix-sept	seventeen
deux	two	dix-huit	eighteen
trois	three	dix-neuf	nineteen
quatre	four	vingt	twenty
cinq	five	vingt et un	twenty-one
six	six	vingt-deux	twenty-two
sept	seven	trente	thirty
huit	eight	quarante	forty
neuf	nine	cinquante	fifty
dix	ten	soixante	sixty
onze	eleven	soixante-dix	seventy
douze	twelve	quatre-vingts	eighty
treize	thirteen	quatre-vingt-dix	ninety
quatorze	fourteen	cent	one hundred
quinze	fifteen	mille	one thousand

Colours

beige	beige	noir, noire	black
blanc, blanche	white	orange	orange
bleu, bleue	blue	rouge	red
brun, brune	brown	vert, verte	green
jaune	yellow	violet, violette	purple

Places

PROVINCES AND TERRITORIES

la Colombie-Britannique	British Columbia	la Nouvelle-Écosse	Nova Scotia
l'Alberta (f.)	Alberta	l'Île-du-Prince-Édouard (f.)	Prince Edward Island
la Saskatchewan	Saskatchewan	Terre-Neuve-et-Labrador	Newfoundland and Labrador
le Manitoba	Manitoba	le Yukon	Yukon
l'Ontario (m.)	Ontario	les Territoires du Nord-Ouest (m., pl.)	Northwest Territories
le Québec	Quebec		
le Nouveau-Brunswick	New Brunswick	le Nunavut	Nunavut

COUNTRIES AND CONTINENTS

l'Afrique (f.)	Africa	la France	France
l'Amérique du Nord (f.)	North America	l'Inde (f.)	India
l'Angleterre (f.)	England	l'Italie (f.)	Italy
l'Australie (f.)	Australia	la Jamaïque	Jamaica
le Brésil	Brazil	le Japon	Japan
le Canada	Canada	le Mexique	Mexico
la Chine	China	la Russie	Russia
les États-Unis (m., pl.)	United States	la Suisse	Switzerland

Verbs

ER VERBS

aimer	to like	jouer	to play
apporter	to bring	manger	to eat
chanter	to sing	montrer	to show
chercher	to look for	penser	to think
danser	to dance	porter	to wear, to carry
demander	to ask	regarder	to watch
donner	to give	rencontrer	to meet
écouter	to listen	rester	to stay
étudier	to study	téléphoner	to phone
fermer	to close	travailler	to work
habiter	to live	trouver	to find

IR VERBS

bâtir	to build	punir	to punish
choisir	to choose	réfléchir	to ponder
finir	to finish	remplir	to fill
grandir	to grow tall	réussir	to succeed
obéir	to obey		

RE VERBS

attendre	to wait for	prendre	to take
défendre	to defend	rendre	to give back, to return something
descendre	to go down	répondre	to answer
entendre	to hear	vendre	to sell
perdre	to lose		

Small Words

WORDS THAT TELL WHERE

au-dessus	above	entre	between
autour	around	ici	here
de	from	là-bas	over there
dedans	inside	loin	far
dehors	outside	partout	everywhere
derrière	behind	près	near
sous	under	voici	here
devant	in front of	voilà	there

WORDS THAT TELL HOW MUCH

assez (de)	enough	plus (de)	more
beaucoup (de)	a lot, many	très	very
moins (de)	less, fewer	trop (de)	too much, too many
un peu (de)	little, few		

WORDS THAT TELL WHEN

aujourd'hui	today	tôt	early
hier	yesterday	bientôt	soon
demain	tomorrow	de bonne heure	early
maintenant	now	enfin	at last, finally
avant	before	ensuite	next
après	after	il y a	ago
tout de suite	now, immediately	longtemps	for a long time
tard	late	puis	then

INTERJECTIONS

Aïe !	Ow!	Oh !	Wow!
Bah !	Bah!	Miam ! Miam !	Mmm! Good!
Ben . . . euh . . .	Well, er . . .	Ouf !	Oof!
Beurk !	Yuck!	Oups !	Oops!
Paf !	Slap!	Pan !	Bang!
Boum !	Boom!	Toc ! Toc !	Knock! Knock!
Hein ?	Eh?	Pouah !	Yuck!

QUESTION WORDS

combien (de)	how many, how much	quand	when
comment	how	que, qu'	what
où	where	qui	who
pourquoi	why		

Appendix 1: Useful Resources

Here are some books and games you might enjoy. You can find them in libraries, at French bookstores, or online.

Some of these books are translations of English books. Knowing the English books will make it easier for you to understand the French ones. You can also use some of the strategies you learned on pages 64–65, such as looking at the pictures, finding words you know and words that look like English words, and reading titles and captions. It may also help to read the books out loud. (Use the Pronunciation Guide on pages 81–83 if you have difficulty.) And don't forget — you can always ask someone to help you, like a friend, an older brother or sister, a neighbour, your parents, or your teacher. Whatever strategies you use, have fun!

500 Jeux Amusants
Published by Éditions Scholastic
This book is filled with mazes, jokes, crossword puzzles, observation games, and many more activities.

À la ferme, Dans la forêt, and Vive le sport !
Published by Éditions quatre fleuves/Éditions Babiroussa
Written by Faustina Fiore
Illustrated by Tony Wolf
Open each case to discover twelve mini-books about different aspects of a theme, from the farm to the forest to the world of sports.

Apprentis lecteurs
Published by Éditions Scholastic
This series includes stories and information books about geography, science, health, and holidays.

Cartes cache mots
Published by Héritage Jeunesse
Learn about opposites and numbers by playing games with these card collections.

Clarice Bean, c'est moi
Published by La courte échelle
Written and illustrated by Lauren Child
In this series of stories, you'll read about Clarice Bean and her often funny family, classmates, and teachers.

Cloé et Alix
Published by Éditions Scholastic
Written by Scott Higgs
Join Cloé and Alix, two best friends, as they play together and search out adventures.

Je peux lire
Published by Éditions Scholastic
This collection includes fictional stories as well as books about math, science, and crafts.

Je veux connaître les éléments
By Etta Kaner
Published by Éditions Scholastic
Practise your weather words in this collection of books about the weather.

Jouons avec Léon
Published by La courte échelle
Written and illustrated by Annie Groovie
A cyclops named Léon explores different themes — from sports to circuses — in each book of the series.

APPENDIX 1: USEFUL RESOURCES

Leapfrog — Tag
Distributed by Le lutin rouge
These stories, based on favourite cartoon characters, are designed for LeapFrog's interactive Tag Reading System.

Le petit Nicolas : Un livre pop-up
Published by Gallimard Jeunesse
Written by René Goscinny
Illustrated by Jean-Jacques Sempé
This pop-up book shows six scenes from stories about Nicolas, a mischievous French boy.

Lire et découvrir
Published by Éditions Scholastic
Written by Melvin and Gilda Berger
Learn about the wonders of nature through the seasons in this series of nonfiction books.

Mammouth Académie
Published by La courte échelle
Written and illustrated by Neal Layton
This series of graphic novels tells about a group of woolly mammoths who are students at Mammoth Academy. There, they learn about the world around them and about the most dangerous creatures of all — humans!

Mots mystères
Published by Éditions Scholastic
Enjoy this book of word searches and other fun activities.

Petit roman
Published by Éditions Scholastic
This series of short novels will make you laugh.

Raconte-moi une histoire
Published by Éditions Scholastic
Follow along in the books as you listen to CDs of stories written by favourite authors, including Robert Munsch, Phoebe Gilman, Barbara Reid, and Gilles Tibo.

Savais-tu ?
Published by Les Éditions Michel Quintin
Learn interesting facts about animals in this series of information books.

Vois-tu ce que je vois ?
Published by Éditions Scholastic
Written and illustrated by Walter Wick
Try to find objects hidden in these photographs.

Dictionaries

Collins First Time French Dictionary
Collins French School Dictionary
Published by HarperCollins Canada

Mon premier dictionnaire illustré de français :
  À l'école   La ville
  La maison   Les vacances
ELI Dictionnaire illustré français – Junior
ELI Dictionnaire illustré français
Published by European Language Institute (ELI)

97

Appendix 2: Answer Key

Page 35
TRY THIS!
(Masculine and Feminine Nouns)
- l'ami, l'amie
  un ours, une ourse

- la porte
  la classe
  le bébé
  le frère
  la dame
  le monsieur
  le mercredi
  l'Ontario (*m.*)
  le tableau
  l'ordinateur (*m.*)
  la maman
  le papa
  l'astronaute (*m.* or *f.*)
  la pomme
  la sœur
  la tante
  le printemps
  la vache

Page 37
TRY THIS!
(Singular and Plural Nouns)
- les pommes
- les chevaux
- des choux
- les mentons
- les mains
- les morceaux
- les neveux
- les métaux
- des Irlandais
- les gaz
- des Français
- les familles Bélanger

Page 39
TRY THIS!
(Subject Pronouns)
- Ils jouent dans le parc.
- Elle parle à son ami.
- Elles regardent un film.
- Ils mangent le petit déjeuner.
- Il court vite.

Page 40

TRY THIS!
(Singular and Plural Adjectives)
- une petite maison
- un grand garçon
- une dame triste
- les chandails rouges
- la porte ouverte
- les grandes écoles

Page 42

Try This!
(Possessive Adjectives)
- mon oncle
- les sœurs de Nicole
- son bâton de hockey
- le livre de la fille
- tes amis or vos amis
- la balle des enfants
- ses patins
- notre mère
- leurs bottes
- la queue de l'éléphant
- le jouet du bébé

Page 48

TRY THIS!
(Infinitive Forms: Common Verbs)
- Nous parlons.
- Tu choisis.
- Je cours.
- Ils entendent le chien.
- Vous attendez votre tour.
- Elle joue du piano.

Page 50

TRY THIS!
(Common Irregular Verbs)
- Elle est intelligente.
- Nous avons un gâteau.
- Vous allez à la bibliothèque.
- Il a douze ans.

Page 51

TRY THIS!
(The Imperative)
- Chantons une chanson.
- Mange tes légumes.
- Écoutez bien.

APPENDIX 2: ANSWER KEY

Page 53

TRY THIS!
(Adverbs)
- Il a beaucoup de bonbons.
- Maman n'a pas assez de biscuits.
- Il marche lentement pour aller chez le dentiste.
- Les élèves vont vite dans la cour d'école.
- Marie joue souvent au volleyball, mais elle joue rarement du piano.

Page 56

TRY THIS!
(Prepositions, Conjunctions, Interjections)
- Miam ! C'est délicieux !
- Julie et Thomas mangent des biscuits.
- J'aime le baseball mais je n'aime pas le soccer.
- Marc va au cinéma avec son père.
- Voilà un livre pour Manon.

Page 58

TRY THIS!
(Making a Sentence Negative)
- The sentence is positive. Il ne parle pas beaucoup.
- The sentence is positive. Vous n'habitez pas sur la rue Lafayette.
- The sentence is negative. Nous mangeons vite.
- The sentence is positive. Je ne nage pas dans la piscine.
- The sentence is negative. Tu achètes le livre.

Page 59

IT'S A WRAP!
(Putting It All Together)

Aïe ! J'ai trop de devoirs.
- Aïe — interjection
- J' — subject
- ai — verb
- trop — adverb
- devoirs — noun

Mon manteau est sous la chaise bleue.
- Mon — possessive adjective
- manteau — subject
- est — verb
- sous — preposition
- la — definite article
- chaise — noun
- bleue — adjective

Je suis très contente parce que je vais chez ma grand-mère.
- Je — subject
- suis — verb
- très — adverb
- contente — adjective
- parce que — conjunction
- je — subject
- vais — verb
- chez — preposition
- ma — possessive adjective
- grand-mère — noun

Quand est-ce que ton père achète une nouvelle auto ?
- Quand est-ce que — question word
- ton — possessive adjective
- père — subject
- achète — verb
- une — indefinite article
- nouvelle — adjective
- auto — noun

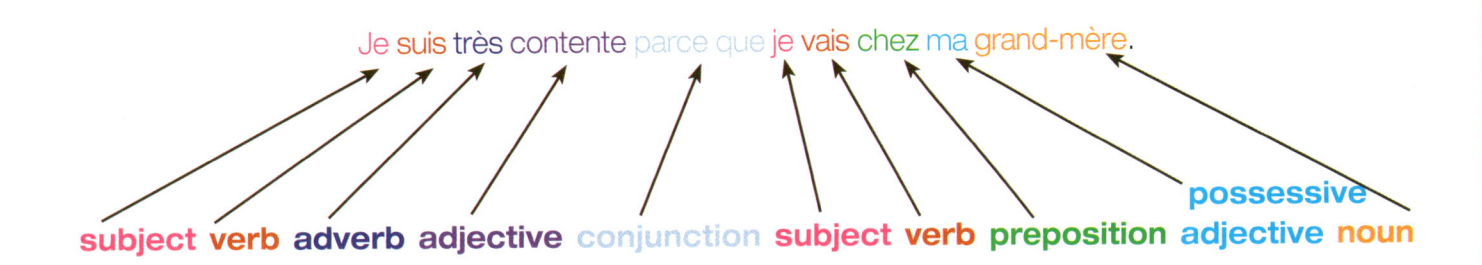

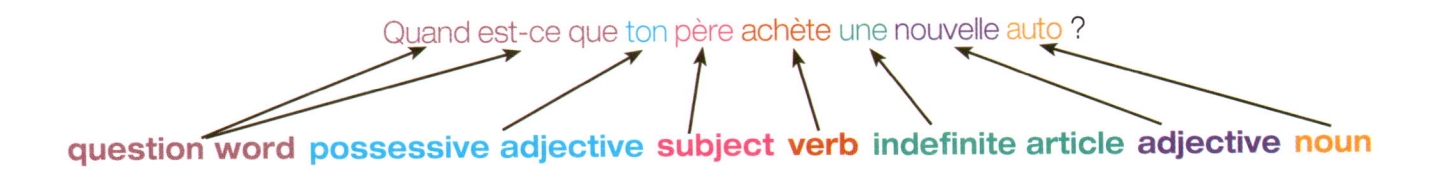

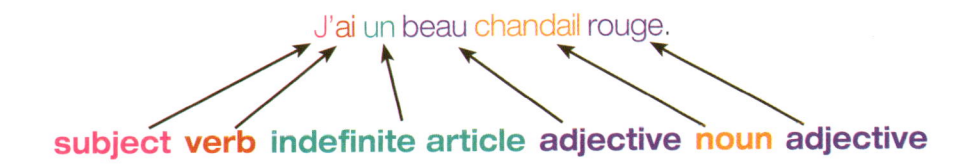

J'ai un beau chandail rouge.
- J' — subject
- ai — verb
- un — indefinite article
- beau — adjective
- chandail — noun
- rouge — adjective

APPENDIX 2: ANSWER KEY

Page 68

TRY THIS!
(Intonation)

- Marcel et son ami Jean-Louis vont au cinéma samedi après-midi.

- Monsieur Duval est notre prof aujourd'hui. Pourquoi ? Est-ce que madame Thériault est malade ?

- C'est dimanche et nous allons chez grand-mère pour souper.

- Ma sœur a un nouveau chandail bleu. Il est très beau.

- Sarah a un nouveau poisson. De quelle couleur est son poisson ?

- Le chien chasse la balle. Il court très vite !

- Au souper, je mange une salade, des spaghettis, du pain et au dessert, de la crème glacée. Ouf ! J'ai trop mangé !

Index

A

abbreviations, 73
Aboriginal peoples, 6, 10, 12
Acadia and Acadians, 4, 5, 11
Acadian World Congress, 11
accents, 24–25
   aigu, 25
   cédille, 25
   circonflexe, 25
   grave, 25
   tréma, 25
adjectives, 40–43, 59
   and adverbs, 52
   feminine, 40
   interrogative, 43
   masculine, 40
   placement, 43
   plural, 40
   possessive, 41–42, 43, 59
   singular, 40
adverbs, 52–53, 59
aigu, l'accent, 25
"À la claire fontaine", 19
ALLER verb, 48–50
"Alouette", 19
alphabet, 23–24
amounts, vocabulary for, 94
anthems, 14
Arbour, Louise, 18
articles, 33, 59, 72
   definite, 33, 59
   indefinite, 33, 59
   partitive, 33
Astérix, 80

Avignon, 21
AVOIR verb, 48, 50

B

baguettes, 13
baked beans with pork, 12
bilingualism, 2
Bombardier company, 19
Bombardier, Joseph-Armand, 19
Bonhomme Carnaval, 9, 10
bonhomme dansant, le, 20
Boucher, Gaétan, 17
Bouctouche, 11
Brassard, Jean-Luc, 17
Brazil, 10

C

Canada
   anthem, 14
   government, 3
   Parliament Hill, 3
   prime ministers, 8
Canadian Broadcasting
   Corporation. *See* Radio-Canada
Canadian explorers, 10
capital cities, 3
capitalization, 31
Caraquet, 4, 11
card games, 20, 80
Carnaval, 9, 10
Carrier, Roch, 14
Cartier, Jacques, 5

cartoons, 80
Catherine, Sainte, 13
CBC. *See* Radio-Canada
CDs, x, 19, 60–63, 79, 97
cédille, la, 25
ceinture fléchée, 10
Champlain, Samuel de, 3
chandail de hockey, Le, 14
cheese, 13
circonflexe, l'accent, 25
Cirque du Soleil, 16
clauses, 55
clothing, vocabulary for, 90
cognates, 64, 66
colonization, 5–7
colons, 56
colours, vocabulary for, 92
comic books, 80
commands, 51
commas, 56
common expressions, 70
common nouns, 31, 34
commonly used words, 84–95
Compagnie de La Vérendrye, La, 10
computer games, 65, 80
Concentration (game), 20, 80
Congo, Democratic Republic of the, 6
Congrès mondial acadien, Le, 11
conjunctions, 55, 59
correspondence, writing of, 78–79
coureurs de bois, 6
Creole, Haitian, 7
crêpes, x, 12
croissants, 13

103

D

days, vocabulary for, 31, 35, 84
definite articles, 33, 59
Despatie, Alexandre, 17
determiners. See articles
Devoir, Le, 65
dictionaries, 35, 70, 72, 73, 97
   commonly used words, 84–95
   visual, 73, 79, 80
Dion, Céline, 14
DVDs, x, 60–63, 79

E

Éditions Scholastic, 65
e-mails, 78
emphasis. See intonation
ER verbs, 44–45, 93
ÊTRE verb, 48–50
exclamation marks, 56
explorers
   Canadian, 10
   French, 3, 5, 6
expressions, common, 70

F

FAIRE verb, 48–50
feminine adjectives, 40
feminine nouns, 32, 34–35
   and adjectives, 40, 41, 43
   and articles, 33
   and prepositions, 42
Festival acadien de Caraquet, Le, 11
Festival du Voyageur, Le, 10
festivals, xi, 9, 10, 13
   Acadian, 4, 11
   winter, 9–10
fête de la Sainte-Catherine, La, 13
fèves au lard, 12
fiddle music, 19
final consonants, 28

fishbones, 74, 75
flags, 5, 11
fleurs-de-lis, 5
foods, x, 12–13
   vocabulary for, 90–91
France, 5–7, 9, 13
Francophones, 2
   ancesters, 5
   history in Canada, 5–6
   immigration, 6
Fréchette, Sylvie, 17
French-Canadian
   artists, 14–16
   astronauts, 18
   athletes, 17
   culture, x, 9–16
   inventors, 19
   justices, 18
   music, 10, 11, 19–20
   patron saints, 10, 11, 13
   songs, 14, 19
   See also festivals; foods
French-English dictionaries, 35, 70, 72, 73
French explorers, 3, 5, 6
French language
   books, 96–97
   games, 20, 70, 65, 80, 96–97
   numbers of speakers of, 5, 7
future tense, 44

G

games, 96–97
   computer, 65, 80
   Concentration, 20, 80
   word, 70, 81
Garneau, Marc, 18
Gaspé Peninsula, 5
Gaultier, Pierre, de Varennes, 10
Gay, Marie-Louise, 14
gender. See feminine nouns; masculine nouns
"Gens du pays", 19
graphic novels, 97

graphic organizers, 62, 74
   fishbones, 74, 75
   KWL (or SVA) charts, 74, 76
   T-charts, 74, 76
   Venn diagrams, 74, 75
   webs, 74, 77
grave, l'accent, 25

H

Haiti, 6, 7
Haitian Creole, 7
Heymans, Emilie, 17
Hockey Sweater, The, 15
holidays, vocabulary for, 85
home and household, vocabulary for, 80, 89–90

I

ID cards, 78
Image Mill, The, 16
immigration, 6, 9
imperative verbs, 51
indefinite articles, 33, 59
infinitive verb forms, 44–48
interjections, 56, 59, 95
   and punctuation, 56
Internet x, 63, 80
interrogative adjectives, 41
intonation, 62, 63, 66, 67–68
IR verbs, 44, 46, 94
irregular verbs, 48–50

J

John the Baptist, Saint, 10

K

Know–Want to Know–Learned (KWL) charts, 74, 76

L

LaFleur, Guy, 17
Lavallée, Calixa, 14
Lemieux, Mario, 17
Lepage, Robert, 16
letter combinations, 26
listening strategies, 60–63, 79–80
location, vocabulary for, 94
loggers, 12
Louisiana, 5, 10, 11
Lucky Luke, 80

M

Magdalen Islands, 5
Manitoba, 6, 10, 93
maple syrup, 12
Mardi Gras, 10
Mary, Saint, 11
mascots, 9, 10
masculine adjectives, 40
masculine nouns, 32, 34–35
   and adjectives, 40, 41, 43
   and articles, 33
   and prepositions, 42
meatball stew, 12
"Mon merle", 19
"Mon pays", 14
months, vocabulary for, 31, 35, 84
Montreal, 4, 13
Montreal Canadiens, 15
music, 10, 11, 19–20
   See also songs

N

negatives, 57–58
neighbourhoods, vocabulary for, 88
New Brunswick, 4, 11, 93
   official languages, 2
   OIF membership, 8
   premiers, 8
   Village Historique Acadien, 5
Newfoundland, 5, 93
newspapers, 65
Northwest Territories, 2, 93
nouns, 31–37, 59
   capitalization, 31
   common, 31, 34
   determiners for, 33
   plural, 36–37, 40, 41, 43
   proper, 31, 62
   singular, 36–37, 43
   See also feminine nouns; masculine nouns
Nova Scotia, 5, 93
numbers, vocabulary for, 33, 92
Nunavut, 2, 93

O

"O Canada", 14
objects, 57
official languages, 2
Oka, 13
Old French, 24
Old Montreal, 4
Ontario, 2, 93
Organisation internationale de la Francophonie (OIF), 8
Ottawa, 3

P

papillottes, 13
parades, 10, 11
Parliament Hill, 3
partitive articles, 33
parts of sentences
   clauses, 55
   negatives, 57–58
   objects, 57
   phrases, 55, 59
   subjects, 57, 59
   See also verbs
parts of speech, 31–59
   adjectives, 40–43, 59
   adverbs, 52–53, 59
   articles, 33, 59, 72
   conjunctions, 55, 59
   interjections, 56, 59, 95
   nouns, 31–37, 59
   prepositions, 42, 54, 59
   pronouns, 38–39
   See also verbs
past tense, 44
patron saints. See saints
pattes de cochon, 12
Payette, Julie, 18
Pays de la Sagouine, Le, 11
pea soup, x, 12
periods, 56
phrases, 55, 59
pigs' feet, 12
Pius X (pope), 10
places, vocabulary for, 93
Plante, Jacques, 17
plural adjectives, 40
plural nouns, 36–37
   and adjectives, 40, 41, 43
   and articles, 33
   and prepositions, 42
podcasts, x, 63, 80
pont d'Avignon, Le, 21
possessive adjectives, 41–42, 43, 59
postcards, 79
poutine, 13
premiers, 8
prepositions, 42, 54, 59
present tense, 44
Presse, La, 65
prime ministers, 8
Prince Edward Island, 5, 93
pronouns, 38–39
pronunciation, 61, 62
   guide, 81–83
   of accents, 25
   of letters, 23–24, 26, 27
   See also intonation
proper nouns, 31, 62
provinces and territories, 2, 3, 8

vocabulary for, 93
See also names of specific provinces and territories
punctuation, 56

Q

Quebec, xi, 3, 6, 19, 93
   cheese, 13
   flag, 5
   official languages, 2
   OIF membership, 8
   premiers, 8
Quebec City, 3
   anniversary, 16
   Carnaval, 9, 10
question marks, 56
question words, 58, 59, 95

R

radio, 60, 63
Radio-Canada, 63, 65
ragoût de boulettes, 12
reading strategies, 64–65, 79–80
reenactors, 10
retrouvailles, Les, 11
RE verbs, 44, 46–47, 94
Richard, Maurice "Rocket", 15, 17
roots and root words, 45–48, 64
Routhier, Adolphe-Basile, 14
Rwanda, 6, 7

S

Saint-Jean-Baptiste, La, 10, 14
saints, 10, 11, 13
Savoir–Veux Savoir–Appris (SVA) charts, 74, 76
school, vocabulary for, 85–86
seasons, vocabulary for, 35, 84
self (About Me), vocabulary for, 87
semi-colons, 56
Senegal, 6

sentences, 57–59
   and question words, 58, 59
   negatives, 57–58
singular adjectives, 40
singular nouns, 36–37
   and adjectives, 43
snowmobiles, 19
soldiers, 10
songs, 14, 19
   See also music
soupe aux pois, x, 12
speaking strategies, 66–71, 79–80
special consonants, 27
special letter combinations, 26
spelling, 72
spoons, playing, 20
sports, vocabulary for, 87
St. Boniface, 6
Stella books, 14
strategic translation, xi
subject pronouns, 38–39
subjects, 57, 59
"Sur le pont d'Avignon", 21
Switzerland, 7
syllables, emphasizing, 67–68

T

taffy, 12, 13
T-charts, 74, 76
television, x, 60, 63, 80
tenses, 44
territories, 2, 93
textbooks, 72
time and duration, vocabulary for, 95
times of day, vocabulary for, 84
Tintamarre, le, 11
Tintin, 80
tire Sainte-Catherine, la, 13
tongue twisters, 28
tourtière, x, 12
tréma, le, 25

V

Varennes, Pierre Gaultier de, 10
Venn diagrams, 74, 75
verbs, 44–50, 57, 59
   and adverbs, 52
   ALLER, 48–50
   AVOIR, 48, 50
   ER verbs, 44–45, 93
   ÊTRE, 48–50
   FAIRE, 48–50
   imperatives, 51
   infinitive forms, 44–48
   IR verbs, 44, 46, 94
   irregular verbs, 48–50
   RE verbs, 44, 46–47, 94
   tenses, 44
   vocabulary for, 93–94
Vietnam, 7
Vieux Québec, 3
Vigneault, Gilles, 14
Village Historique Acadien, 5
Villeneuve, Gilles, 17
Villeneuve, Jacques, 17
visual dictionaries, 73, 79, 80
"V'là l'bon vent", 19
vocabulary, 72, 73, 80
   building, 66, 70, 81–95
   commonly used words, 84–95
vowels, 24–25
voyageurs, 6, 10

W

weather, vocabulary for, 85
webs, 74
websites, 65
Winnipeg, 10
winter carnivals, 9–10
word games, 70–71
writing strategies, 72–80

Author Biography

Marie Turcotte's long professional career has all been spent in FSL. She taught French, French Immersion and Histoire at the secondary level for many years. Later, Marie was Program Development Manager at Copp Clark Ltd., Managing Editor at Pearson Education, Editor-in-Chief, FSL, at Gage, Senior Consultant at Thomson Nelson, and Director of Marketing at RK Publishing.

Currently Marie is a freelancer working from her home in Ontario. She continues to work with French teachers across the country and conduct workshops on the latest trends in FSL teaching.